Thinking About Innovation

John L. Gordon

AKRI Limited

First Edition 2008

Published by AKRI Limited
Registered in England: 5362927

Registered Address
19 Windlebrook Crescent, Windle, St.Helens
Merseyside. WA10 6DY

Web Site: www.akri.co.uk

ISBN: 978-0-9560632-0-5

Printed by
Rhodes Printing
Boundary Road, St.Helens WA10 2QA. UK Telephone 01744 697300

Contents:

Acknowledgements:

This book was written independently between 2006 and 2008. However, the information contained within it is based on a considerable and varied set of influences. I have attempted to list as many of these influences as I can at the end of the book under the heading 'Sources and Influences'. However, it is particularly important to mention the experiences gained through involvement with several projects carried out in Blackburn and the involvement of a core industrial group that helped to guide and monitor these projects.

The Innovation projects were hosted and managed by the Senior Staff and Principalship at Blackburn College between 1990 and 2004.
Many of the Specific projects were also supported by Blackburn Borough Council.
Specific funding organisations for a range of projects that have had influence include:
- European ADAPT Project + European Partners
- European ESF Funding
- European ERDF Funding
- UK DTI Support and Funding

The core industrial group that helped to direct and manage the work on innovation provided help with all aspects of the work and on all projects although the composition of the group changed a little over the years. Particular thanks should go to Rolls-Royce, BAE Systems, Akzo Nobel, and Worswick Engineering who offered help for the entire duration of all of the work.

These specific acknowledgements should not detract from the valuable support offered by many other people and groups. A more complete list is available at the end of this book.

Thinking about Innovation
John L. Gordon – December 2006 – September 2008

Introduction

This book will encourage thought about organisational innovation. The primary aim of the work is to help an organisation to improve its performance by realising benefit derived from innovation. Innovation itself is discussed openly and in depth, but the goals of enhanced innovation are clear and unambiguous as are the plans for action that an organisation may derive from experiences of this work.

An early contributor to the thoughts that have ultimately produced this work is an in depth study of knowledge, intelligence and innovation itself, carried out by the author. Some of the insights are derived from a three year European funded ADAPT programme to study innovation in business. The project was managed by Blackburn College and supported by many large and small organisations including Rolls-Royce plc, BAE Systems, Akzo Nobel, Worswick Engineering and many more. Experts were consulted in a range of disciplines including business managers, directors, sports coaches, medical specialists and business advisors. This project looked critically at what those involved with innovation actually thought about it.

Mentioning company contribution like this hides the considerable influence that many individuals exerted on the way that the thoughts behind this work were formed. Many of those individuals becoming friends that were happy to criticise early thoughts in a real desire to influence progress and identify weaknesses. Some of these influences came from specific trips and lengthy discussion with people that had a very strong opinion and considerable experience in the area. Influence also came from the small group within Blackburn College that worked on Innovation Projects and the valued support given to us by the Chief Executive and her staff.

The study of intelligence formed a global framework for the focus on innovation. A detailed interest in both artificial and human intelligence guided much of the exploration that was carried out during several research phases. This contributed to the way that the thoughts derived from various innovation studies were developed for this more global work. The influence of the rigour and insights involved in the study of Artificial Intelligence helped to develop a critical view of the complexities of Innovation.

At the heart of the exploration of innovation was knowledge and a strong desire to understand what people would need to know in order to develop an environment where innovation flourishes. An important part of this was a Knowledge Study project carried out at BAE Systems to investigate Continuous Improvement in an advanced manufacturing cell. This project was rewarding because it provided an opportunity to carry out a focussed and in depth investigation of what needed to be known and done for continuous improvement to be achieved.

I am most grateful for the influences of the late Robert Muller (Bob) who led Artificial Intelligence related work in Digital (UK) for many years and then later worked towards the formation of a national organisation for Creativity. He helped me to forge my own views about Creativity and Innovation so that both concepts could live comfortably alongside each other in this work.

The book begins with a discussion and works towards the development of policy. The discussion attempts to mirror the influences and opinions that helped the work to develop. Discussion does not claim any moral high ground for those that would disagree. It simply attempts to show how policy was formed by exploring the various ideas and opinions that helped the work to mature. Beginning this work on innovation with a section called 'discussion' is part of the attempt to help organisations and individuals see that innovation is something that should come from within. The experiences and opinions of the individual and the organisation are not irrelevant to the development of the correct process of innovation for a particular organisation.

Once the debate concerning innovation is opened up, it is then time to decide what is actually meant by innovation and to decide what a successful innovation scheme should deliver. As with the discussion, it is useful to refer to the opinions of others but also remember that it is the opinion of the drivers of the specific organisation that are ultimately important. The section on innovation is intended to help individuals and the organisation to be clear about what they think innovation is and what it should bring.

When the meanings are clear, it is time to take a first look at the creation of a process for innovation. Innovation is something that needs to be done and the framework for the activities involved needs to be thought out. It is also useful, when looking at a process for innovation, to begin to consider the barriers that the process will meet and how to overcome those barriers. Such thought processes will help a working innovation scheme to recognise and overcome new barriers that may be met in the future.

Business culture is relevant to all business activity but above all, to innovation. If the culture is not right, then innovation may never work properly. Unfortunately, business culture is not an easy thing to deal with and attitudes of all staff, including and in particular, the most senior staff may need to be considered. The discussion and exploration of culture within this work is intended to help an organisation to begin to grow a truly supportive culture within the business. This effort is likely to benefit the whole business but it is an essential part of innovation.

In order to assess the effectiveness of a developing innovation policy, innovation itself needs to be assessed or measured. Assessing innovation needs to be tackled if the innovation scheme is to continue to improve. The section on assessing innovation considers several ways of doing this and introduces the fundamental issues that an organisation needs to think about when assessing its own innovation scheme. Initially, several ways of looking at organisations with respect to how innovative they are at the time, are considered. These assessment tools not only show how innovative an organisation is but also suggest ways that it can improve. The goals of innovation assessment or measurement change when there is a particular innovation scheme in operation. The goals are now more closely aligned with business monitoring and management.

The final step in the series of steps towards a successful innovation scheme is dealt with in the section on managing innovation. This section recognises that even the best of schemes, if left alone, will grind slowly, or maybe not so slowly, to a stop. This is particularly true for a scheme that could be considered to be outside the primary business functional areas; a sort of added benefit but we could do without it. This step is where all of the previous steps need to be brought together and made to work successfully over the long term. Without good innovation management, an innovation scheme will not work. The sustainability of projects can be a constant battle in business and this is particularly true for innovation.

There are many other things that are worth considering within the context of a successful innovation scheme but the main issues have been dealt with in the six sections of this work. The following point should be carefully noted however.

This work is intended to help an organisation to create the best and most successful innovation scheme that it can do. It is not intended to provide a blueprint but it is intended to show the way. There is probably no blueprint that will suit every organisation and it should be recognised that those that know the organisation best, the ones within it, are probably the best people to create the very best innovation scheme for that particular organisation. This work is intended to help them do just that.

One final introductory point is to again recognise that the thoughts and opinions of many people have influenced this work. Even where I, the author, can claim, to have written it several years after the end of direct influences, the things that have been written are a fusion of a great many ideas that have come from a broad range of sources and experiences. Bringing them all together to consider a workable innovation scheme is not a trivial task. The difference between understanding the parts of an innovation scheme and understanding a complete and integrated scheme is almost as great as the difference between knowing how to create and manage a successful innovation scheme and actually doing it.

1. Discussion

This first chapter contains more general discussion around innovation and related concepts. It is intended to provide the reader with some of the background thoughts that have been derived from interviews, discussion, analysis, reflection, design and testing. Subsequent chapters will cite only opinion, design, analysis etc that are relevant to the particular issue of the chapter. In this first chapter however, things will be discussed much more openly and less formally. Most of this discussion is recalled from several innovation studies that took place between 1990 and 2003.

There is some repetition within this discussion because suggestions offered in one context can be usefully tested in another context. The things that people may say about innovation and the things that they may agree with or disagree with can be influenced by the context within which the discussion takes place.

There have been no more than about twenty people from various sectors that have contributed to the more formal interview process. In defence of this small population, these people were chosen for their potential to contribute to the programme and were each expert in their field and directly involved with innovation in some form or another. In addition, several of the people from within this population made contributions to the design and development of the thoughts and systems that emerged from the work. After this defence, it is worth stating that there have been many more people based around the UK and in Austria and Germany that have contributed to the thoughts and opinions expressed here regarding innovation. Within the UK, people from other related projects have made contributions. Within Europe, people directly involved in their own national innovation schemes and collaborating in an international framework have made contributions.

It is fair to say that my own thoughts, my own background and my strong attachment to the studies of Knowledge and Intelligence (particularly Artificial Intelligence) have greatly influenced this discussion. That and the fact that this work is being created several years after the formal studies on Innovation were begun and after the initial innovation products were created and after these products have been tried and tested, also creates a significant influence. I must admit that an on going desire to consider what needs to be known for undertakings, with regard to the promotion of innovation and the echoes of a Director at Rolls-Royce who constantly raised the 'So What' issue with respect to business, have also had a significant impact on these thoughts and idea as have my own on going business related studies of knowledge and intelligence.

Now that a context has been established, it is probably time to begin to look at the discussion and ideas themselves. The reader may agree with many of the opinions expressed, may disagree with them or may have some other thoughts related to them. This is really the point of discussing innovation. It is not as if we can create a formulae or mathematical model that we can use to build and promote innovation in organisations. We must adapt good practice to make it suit the special circumstances of our own environments. It helps therefore to discuss innovation and listen to the ideas of others.

1.1 Early Discussion

A number of years ago (my report written in 1996) the DTI ran an Intelligent Systems Integration Programme (ISIP) and I was the organiser of one of the regional Technology Transfer groups. There were other regional groups and one of the main jobs of these groups was to recruit organisational participation. I remember at one early meeting, announcing that the North West had almost 40 member organisations and thought that this was a small number although it was very difficult to achieve larger numbers. I was interested when most other regions announced that they had hardly any members from industry. The odd thing was that at the next meeting, about 3 months later, one group announced that it now had over one hundred members and at the next meeting again, about another three months later, it was back down to hardly any. There was no innovation to be identified here, only a different way of classifying members. After the second meeting, there was a serious need identified for some innovation within the other groups that had not greatly increased their membership, including my own. However, on reflection, at the time, the task simply seemed unattainable and this belief was supported at the next meeting.

Resulting from this issue of membership, there emerged a serious debate amongst the regional group organisers concerning how industrial participation could be engaged. I remember one organiser pointing out that she would note the names and contact details of companies when she was in traffic hold ups in the morning and evening. These contacts may be on buildings or on lorries or on busses. That seemed to be quite innovative at the time.

The ISIP project itself, or at least the regional group part of it, aimed to encourage organisations to adopt intelligent systems into their working framework. At the time an intelligent system may have been an Expert System or a Case Based Reasoning System. This lead to the problem, for groups seeking participation at least, that organisations would be more likely to participate in things that they could identify a direct need for in their business. Unfortunately, we were trying to introduce new ideas, that many organisations had not heard of, and these had not been identified as a need within most organisations. Neither was it a case of organisations waiting for new ideas to come along so that they could evaluate them. The problem was that the companies or organisations had quite enough to deal with as it was and whilst they may find time to participate in something that could be shown to be directly and currently relevant, they were not as likely to participate in things that were completely new and therefore things that may not be relevant.

My 1996 report contained the following few lines:

The name 'Artificial Intelligence' is not attractive to companies. The subject areas covered by 'Artificial Intelligence' are highly relevant and have proven track records. A dichotomy exists with technology transfer with the following opposing views:
1) We should give companies what they want.   (there is an implication contained
2) We should tell companies about new things.   within this dichotomy)

- *If we give companies what they want we are more certain that there will be a good response from the initiative and success, measured by this response, is more certain.*
- *If we tell companies about things that they don't know about, they are less likely to see these things as relevant or needed.*

Early cases like this identified a clear need for innovation in the Technology Transfer arena. One of the ways that this was tackled at the time was by the introduction of collaborative projects. It was quite difficult to get organisations to release staff to participate in a collaborative project but if the project could be shown to be relevant to the organisation then some small level of participation was possible. In our case, in the North West region of England we identified energy as something of common interest and this did indeed generate some participative involvement. We actually addressed the Energy Savings (Energy Efficiency) issue using an Expert System so we satisfied the aims of the programme, although this was delivered outside the programme but still with DTI support. The main point of this however was that several people from several companies got together from time to time to collaborate in the creation of an Expert System that would advise people in organisations about Energy Saving measures that they could adopt. As far as Technology Transfer was concerned, this was a great success because the participating staff all took information about Expert Systems and energy efficiency back to their companies with them as well as ideas derived from other participants. As it happens, the idea of using Energy Efficiency for this purpose had other benefits which I will not go into here other than to say that this innovative idea lead to more benefits than the one it was intended to address. Anyone intrigued by this should find out about the EMMA Energy Efficiency software developed for the Energy Efficiency Office around 1996.

1.2 Discussion from Company Meetings
In addition to interviews about Innovation with individuals, on more than one occasion, meetings of several people from a particular organisation were structured to elicit opinion from a group of people and also to encourage staff from that organisation to review their own thoughts on innovation. In one case, the company had an innovation scheme and used the meeting to share their experiences with me and to discuss the progress of their scheme.

The senior staff member of the organisation was keen to point out that the company had an innovation award at the heart of its innovation programme. Some time was used to explain the details of the award, what it was intended to achieve and how it worked. The generation of ideas were seen to be the starting point and a critical factor for innovation. It was stated that if a manager of an area could not encourage at least one idea from the staff in their charge during each full year, then there was something going wrong. This statement lead to at least one interesting observation concerning a particular area of the company. This area employed 150 managers and the staff in their charge. The area was asked to submit a proposal for a target for the generation of ideas in each year. The senior managers of the area submitted a target of 60 ideas each year as their goal. This was rejected because, with 150 managers, it was considered that at least 150 ideas would be a more reasonable target to aim for. It is interesting to see in this case that a more general statement of intent like the idea that every manager should be able to encourage at least one idea from his or her staff in one year, can lead to tangible guidelines for the development of an innovation scheme.

It was clear that the senior managers in this organisation had been exposed to innovation development workshops or courses themselves. They were familiar with the ideas and use of things like brainstorming, lateral thinking, thinking 'out of the box' etc. They were also clear that their role was to promote innovation rather than be the innovators. Whilst it was recognised that large scale influential ideas leading to innovation were desirable, it was acknowledged that most of the innovation within their organisation comes from many small or even simple ideas. It was stated that the net effect of many small 'innovations' meant significant changes to the business.

It was recognised that the business culture was a major factor in innovation and the most significant aspect of this was the 'Culture of Blame'. It was stated that managers needed to learn to 'bite their tongue' when hearing about mistakes instead of reacting the way they would normally react. Other cultural issues, such as 'that's my job', were discussed but the culture of blame was seen as the single most influential aspect that affected innovation. Control of blame was seen to be something that needed to ripple down from the top. Cultural improvement in business was also recognised as a long term goal.

The major elements of innovation seen at the company were 'creativity', 'motivation' and 'implementation'. It was deliberately pointed out that the company used the term 'implementation' instead of 'exploitation'. Motivation was certainly seen as a significant contributor to innovation. Creativity was seen as something that some people would be better at than others. Whilst it was accepted that creativity in individuals could improve with help and support, it was also recognised that some people are in a higher band of creative ability than others.

The meeting also discussed knowledge as being an important factor in innovation and recognised that some training may actually repress innovation. However, it was stated that staff must be able to undertake training and yet still contribute to innovation by generating ideas.

Whilst this meeting did give some attention to implementation as a key and necessary element in innovation, most of the time of the meeting was devoted to discussing the creative aspects of innovation.

1.3   Discussion from Collaborative Meetings
Collaborative meetings involved people from different organisations getting together to discuss a common topic, in this case, innovation. Some of the meetings were organised to discuss the on going development of innovation projects but others were organised simply to discuss innovation in an open forum with no pre-conceptions or goals.

1.3.1 Open Meeting
During one of the more open meetings, people commented on previous innovation initiatives in their places of work and stated that these tended to focus on exploitation, or implementation, as used in the previous section. Whilst there were good reasons for this, it was clear from discussion that the people themselves found the idea generation and creative aspects of innovation more interesting and probably more critical to successful innovation. The business end of innovation would certainly be in the profitable use of ideas but without ideas in the first place there would be nothing to implement. However, it was noted that the two are

very closely linked. For instance, a flow of ideas would probably soon dry up if it became clear that nothing was ever done with them. Backing for good ideas is one of the factors that help to ensure that ideas are generated.

During open discussion a question was asked about whether unsuccessful ideas can be considered to be innovative. A number of cases were discussed with reference to this point including the fact that the designer of the Tay Bridge received an award just before the bridge blew down in strong winds. The British 'HOTOL' aircraft project was considered to be a significant innovation but it never got off the drawing board. The innovative idea of feeding processed animal protein to cattle was also discussed.

It was claimed at the meeting that in one large company, a particular scheme aimed at generating ideas, actually generated 1800 ideas. Effort was used to reduce these ideas to the best 20 and these ideas were presented to the company executive. This is where the whole process stopped. There was an unwillingness at this point to commit to any action.

It was pointed out that in many cases it is 'RISK' that is the reason that ideas are rejected. Taking action to implement an idea will have a risk associated with it. This risk would almost certainly involve cost but there could be other risks involved. Rejecting ideas means that the potential risks associated with the idea are removed.

Discussion time was given to the role of external influences in company innovation. For instance, national and local regulations can affect what a company can do or the way that it can do it. Certain regulations may cause companies problems and they may need to identify innovative solutions. It was stated that some companies, particularly smaller companies, must innovate to survive. Maybe where larger companies can invest in more efficient production, smaller companies without the investment capital may need to find other ways to remain competitive. Whilst regulations could provide a stimulus for innovation they could also suppress innovation. In the UK, the desire to reduce car exhaust emissions lead to the regulation that cars must be fitted with catalytic converters. This regulation suppressed innovation regarding the development of better ways to reduce car emissions.

There was quite a bit more discussion concerning what innovation was in terms of whether things should be considered innovative. For instance the more general comment, if you lose more than I gain, is that considered successful?

1.3.2 A Focused Meeting
Yet another meeting was a little more focused and involved more people from more companies. The purpose of the meeting was to consider and agree a set of guiding statements to help focus subsequent interviews on Innovation and Motivation. A review of the statements arising from the discussion follows:

The Concept of Innovation:
The scale of innovation is important and companies should not expect regular large-scale innovation but should expect regular small-scale innovation. Small-scale innovation is cumulative and it is environment dependent. What is innovation in one environment may not be in another and innovation is certainly a relative term. Ideas are an important part of innovation but this includes the novel application of existing ideas and it is important that ideas are carried forward to implementation stage to be considered innovative. Innovation may occur spontaneously and not result from a planned programme.
Innovation represents a challenge to custom and practice. It results from the use of initiative and the recognition of opportunities and their conversion into application. Creativity and invention are important components of innovation. Some innovation can result from naïve observation but much of it requires knowledge. Expertise is not innovation and it need not be experts who innovate. Innovation represents a higher plane than knowledge or expertise.

In general it is not accepted that there is more than one type of innovation. Innovation is not like other intellectual activities such as design.

Innovation Environment:
There are several things that can stifle or prevent innovation; the most serious of these things is the existence of a culture of blame within an organisation. Other things that can have a direct influence on innovation include team composition, regulations and even pricing policy. It is important that senior staff create an environment for innovation, this may be more important than being innovative themselves. An expressive atmosphere encourages innovation but potential innovators must be sure that their ideas will be taken seriously. Staff should have a positive attitude and should be allowed to experiment without fear of blame.
Creativity, motivation and implementation are all part of the innovation process. Many people have the capacity to be innovative but it is necessary to have the correct environment to unlock this capacity. Innovation across organisational boundaries or from outside of the organisation can inject new ideas to established practice. Often, the greatest innovative leaps come from unknowledgeable sources from outside of the main stream of activity. Wars (commercial wars) promote or accelerate innovation.

Experts may not be the main innovators and innovation is not caused by any one element such as access to information sources.

The Process of Innovation:
Risks may not be a fundamental part of the innovation process but risk can cause the rejection of innovative ideas. In general, gut feeling often takes the place of risk analysis.
The process of innovation may result from external influences or from problems. Next comes the process of ideas generation, ideas are the starting point for innovation. Ideas may involve small steps or massive leaps or they may result from accidental discovery. The removal of constraints helps the generation of ideas. Ideas may come from a knowledgeable source or may come from a naïve source. It is then important that ideas are acted upon. Good ideas should generate sufficient backing. Ideas that coincide with specific need are more likely to be developed. Good ideas must be identified and acted upon. Opportunities combined with a positive attitude and good practice supports the process of innovation.

Ways of Promoting Innovation:
Brainstorming is a tried and tested method for the promotion of innovation within an organisation. The generation of ideas should be encouraged and any inhibitions that could form a barrier to the process of generating ideas, should be identified and reduced. When teams are required to innovate, personality clash should be avoided. Innovation is driven by need.

Innovative People:
The free child comes out in innovative people when they are generating ideas. Innovation is not a transferable skill but it is desirable that all staff should be innovative to some extent. It is incorrect to say that any particular working group is not innovative.

Innovative Organisations:
Innovation is a vital component for the survival of many companies. Innovation should start with senior staff, who should take ownership of problems. All staff should be involved in the culture of innovation. Changes in business culture such as the elimination of blame can take a long time. Organisations can often be affected by national or international regulations. These can affect the need to innovate.

Innovation and Education:
Although knowledge is an important factor in innovation, formal qualifications are not necessary in innovative people. Education and training can help innovation but some people are naturally more creative than others. Innovation can be developed in staff by teaching skills such as lateral thinking. Education can also help in the identification of barriers to innovation. This results from a recognition that the nature of innovation and what it means to an organisation can be taught even though innovation itself cannot. The role of education and training in innovation forms a complex relationship. It could be argued that education and training can dull innovation.

The Goals of Innovation:
The main effect of innovation is a change in practice and in attitude. Innovation can help sub-contracting companies to own more of their own destiny. Innovation does not lead to staff reductions.

1.4 Individual Interviews

During one project, eleven individual focused interviews were conducted with people in senior management from various industries, in sport, in medicine and in marketing. Interviews were conducted using a central theme for discussion but were not so controlled that they prevented more open comment. This was done to help to focus interviews and create a common theme for them but also to allow individual novel experiences to be expressed. In this project, interviews were analysed with a view of capturing clear statements that were common to all or many interviews. These statements were then returned to each interviewee who marked each as to whether they agreed or disagreed with the statements. In the text below, I have captured only those statements that were either strongly supported or strongly rejected.

For each issue raised below, there is a table of ticked statements that identify the statements that were met with agreement, with those attracting the most agreement appearing at the top of the list. Most of those asked did express an opinion for each of these statements and no more than one person disagreed with the statement in each case.

Some of the issues raised include a few statements that attracted the strongest disagreement. In each case, if there is a second list, the issue receiving the strongest disagreement appears at the top of the list and no more than two people actually agreed with any statement.

1.4.1 Clarifying or Defining Innovation

The definition or clarification of innovation was the area where most statements were extracted, 30 statements in all. Of these, 11 statements received most agreement and 2 met with strong disagreement.

- ✓ Many small scale innovations can have a large impact
- ✓ Innovation may be different in different environments
- ✓ Novel application of existing ideas is innovative
- ✓ Innovation is a relative concept
- ✓ Some of the best innovations are not planned
- ✓ Innovation is a challenge to custom and practice
- ✓ Large scale innovations are infrequent
- ✓ Innovation is using initiative
- ✓ Innovation is recognising an opportunity
- ✓ Innovation is creativity & invention
- ✓ Innovation is converting opportunity

The statements seem to show that people acknowledge that innovation may be different in different environments but the statements seem to all imply that innovation is achieving something based on a new idea.

Whilst people do seem to acknowledge the variability of innovation they are not willing to accept that there are two distinct types of innovation as seen in the list below.

- × Innovation is similar to design
- × There are 2 sorts of innovation, Product and Process

Many cite TRIZ within the context of innovation but the people consulted here do not see design as being similar to innovation.

1.4.2 The Environment for Innovation

There were 22 statements in total concerning the environment for innovation and 11 of these were strongly supported by those completing the feedback form. It seems that people are clearer about what is meant by an environment for innovation than they are about what innovation actually is. This is probably a good result since most of those involved with this work were people that would be responsible for encouraging innovation in others.

- ✓ A culture of BLAME must be eliminated for innovation to flourish
- ✓ Team composition can affect innovation
- ✓ Regulations can force innovation
- ✓ Regulations can suppress innovation
- ✓ Company staff must have a positive attitude to innovation
- ✓ Innovation takes place in an expressive atmosphere
- ✓ Creativity - Motivation – Implementation are all necessary for an innovative environment
- ✓ Many people can innovate: it is the environment which unlocks innovation
- ✓ Ideas must be taken seriously
- ✓ Staff must be allowed to experiment
- ✓ Pricing policy can affect innovation

The statements attracting the most support are quite varied, possibly indicating that people believe that establishing an environment that will encourage innovation to take place is not necessarily straightforward. Certainly, the item at the top of this list is seen as a critical factor for innovation by many people.

- × The internet is an important component of innovation
- × Includes experts

The statement concerning the internet came from one particular interview but most of the people involved disagreed that the internet is an important component of innovation. They also disagreed that innovation is about experts.

1.4.3 The Process of Innovation

There were 17 statements concerning the process of innovation, 12 of which met with significant agreement. However, none of the 17 statements were strongly disagreed with. This list shows that most of the statements that were collected from individuals, find support amongst the large majority of those interviewed. Managers with a responsibility to promote innovation are inclined to think of process as a way to encourage potential innovators.

- ✓ Risk causes ideas to be rejected
- ✓ External influences force innovation
- ✓ Problems can lead to innovation if staff have the correct attitude
- ✓ Ideas are the starting point for innovation
- ✓ The process of ideas generation is critical
- ✓ Generating backing for ideas is important
- ✓ Leaps can be made by removing constraints from the ideas process
- ✓ Accidental discovery can lead to important innovation
- ✓ Risks may need to be taken to promote innovation
- ✓ Innovation does not have to be a high risk process
- ✓ Naivety can be a strength in innovation.
- ✓ Ideas must be acted upon to encourage innovation

It is interesting to see the association of risk with the process of innovation. Clearly the people interviewed were looking at the whole process of innovation and the risks involved with implementation.

1.4.4 Ways of Promoting Innovation

There were only 8 statements generated about ways of promoting innovation and only 4 of these received significant agreement. This list shows that there were relatively fewer ideas elicited from interviewees about direct ways of promoting innovation.

- ✓ Brainstorming sessions
- ✓ Encourage the generation of ideas
- ✓ Ideas are promoted when inhibition is reduced
- ✓ Personality clash can prevent innovation

1.4.5 Innovative People

There were 9 statements in total about innovative people but only 1 of these attracted significant agreement.

- ✓ The 'free child' comes out during innovation

However, there were 3 of the 9 statements that people significantly disagreed with and the statement that accountants are not innovative attracted the strongest disagreement of all with nobody supporting it, even the originator of it, possibly because it was then seen outside the context of the interview.

- × Accountants are not innovative
- × Some people should not be innovative
- × Innovation is a transferable skill

It is interesting to note that people generally agree that innovation is NOT a transferable skill. This must have some impact on the way those managers encourage innovation.

1.4.6 Innovative Organisations

Of the 15 statements concerning innovative organisations, only 4 of them received significant agreement and none of them were strongly rejected.

- ✓ Some companies must innovate to survive
- ✓ National regulations can affect company innovation
- ✓ Cultural changes take many years in business
- ✓ ALL staff must be involved in cultural change

It is interesting to note that two of the statements above refer to an organisational culture. It seems to be generally accepted that culture is a major element in innovation and also that culture is difficult to change.

1.4.7 Innovation and Education

11 statements concerned innovation and education and 7 of these were met with significant agreement. Only 1 of the statements was rejected.

- ✓ Some people are naturally more creative than others
- ✓ Formal qualifications are not necessary for innovation
- ✓ Knowledge is an important factor in innovation
- ✓ One way to develop innovation is to teach lateral thinking
- ✓ Education can help innovation
- ✓ Training can help innovation
- ✓ Barriers to innovation can be identified through education

The idea that knowledge and education play an important part in innovation seems to be the position taken by the people concerned with this project.

- × Innovation can be taught

In contrast with the idea that knowledge and education are important in innovation, it is not accepted that innovation itself can be taught.

1.4.8 Achievements of Innovation

Regarding the achievements of innovation, only 4 statements were collected from interview data. One of these was supported and one rejected. Neither of the statements is particularly revealing other than the observation that managers are looking for change from innovation and they are keen to point out that staff do not need to fear innovation.

- ✓   Innovation causes changes in practice

- ✗   Innovation encourages staff reduction

1.5   Memorable Comment

Almost all of the comment made in group and individual interviews was useful in helping to formulate an approach to innovation. However, it is worth pointing out the one or two statements that seemed to me to be highly thought provoking. These statements left a lasting impression and possibly had a disproportionate influence on my eventual conclusions.

1.5.1 Motivating in Extreme Circumstances

The first of these statements was made within the medical domain by a person responsible for physiotherapy in a large hospital. The interview primarily concerned motivation in this case with innovation being the context within which questions were asked. At first, the person was reluctant to take part in the interviews claiming that she would, in comparison, have little to contribute, but eventually agreed to take part.

As she explained how motivation was used for both staff and patients and what things worked well and what things did not seem to work or worked as de-motivators, she casually explained that one of the difficult parts of this work was motivating patients that had been told they had little time left to live. My immediate reaction was one of astonishment that motivation was even possible in such cases and if it was, how the person responsible for motivating such a patient must be extremely skilled and knowledgeable. Processes and practice concerning this sort of motivation were explained to me and alongside this, what benefits a patient might experience.

There were many valuable points made during this interview but the lasting memory of it was overshadowed by this particular revelation concerning the motivation of terminally ill patients. I left the hospital thinking that the work I was doing was sort of trivial by comparison, by comparison that is, to a person's work that stated that they would have little of value to contribute to my work. It also spurred me to the belief that if this person could do what she was doing, then motivation and innovation in business and industry was not only possible, it was a certainty.

As I write this, eight years after the interview, I do so from memory even though I have the interview notes to hand. Of course, when I refer to the notes after writing the above, I note that the majority of the interview concerned very practical issues that were very valuable in developing the motivational part of this innovation programme. The reference to incurable patients seemed to stop me taking notes at the time and caused me to simply listen to what was being said. However, at least I have the record that it did take place.

Probably the main benefit for me of that specific memory of the interview was, if you can do that, then surely I can do this.

1.5.2 Innovation without end

Another highly significant memory from the interview programme concerned innovation in the sports domain. The person I interviewed was the head coach of a highly successful Rugby League team and although he did talk at length about motivation, this specific memory concerned innovation. Again, I can write about this idea some eight years after the interview, from memory, even though I have the interview notes to hand. However, I have again confirmed that my memories are correct but in the realms of innovation and motivation it is often the impression that ideas give that is important since this impression is what motivates the person with the memories, not the facts.

The statement about innovation came near the end of the interview when a lot of highly relevant issues had been raised and discussed. The statement was about the need for constant and frequent innovation. It was claimed that a top Rugby League team needed to have a weekly turnaround for innovative ideas that is equivalent to about a year in industry. An innovative new play may make a significant difference to a particular game. However, once it has been used, the team to be faced next week are likely to be ready for that play and be able to counter it.

This does not mean that innovative ideas are only used once and then discarded. They can be used again if they are rested. In the mean time, new ideas must replace the previous innovation and success or failure depends significantly on these innovative ideas. The need for innovation is pressing and the rate demanded for innovation is punishing.

Clearly the people responsible for innovation of this sort, like this head coach for a world class Rugby League team, must have a well understood, tried and tested process for generating innovative ideas. Some of these were explained during the interview but it was not until this final statement that the demands of the situation showed that innovation and success were so closely related.

It is also true of this memory that it leaves the impression that if some people can do this with innovation because they are forced to by the demands of their job, then surely business and industry can produce business changing innovation on a regular basis that will create an environment of success.

1.5.3 Measuring Performance
There were a number of other memorable statements made during this investigative phase and I suppose one that maybe less memorable but that struck me as being a key factor for innovation concerned measurement. It was discussed by a person in marketing who was responsible for marketing a sport (not the same sports club as previously discussed).

The statement was made again, at the end of the interview after considerable discussion concerning how to innovate in the marketing of the sports club and how to motivate those involved. The point being made was that all of the innovative changes and all of the improvements in motivation were worth little unless it could be shown that they make a difference. This person was quite clear about what needed to be measured in order to evaluate innovation and had selected very practical things to measure that were significant indicators of success.

It is possible to think of many indicators that one could try to measure, such as the opinion of supporters or the number attending matches etc but the two indicators chosen were gate receipts and shop sales. Any innovative marketing and/or attempt to motivate staff and supporters should be reflected in either or both of the two indicators. If this is not the case then no matter how good the innovation is in other terms, it would not be achieving what the club needed in order to prosper.

If innovation is to be taken seriously in an organisation and it is to be a long term commitment then it is essential that the effort is reflected in success and that this success and therefore the effort can be measured. If this is not done then successful innovation will be difficult to separate from unsuccessful innovation and longer term attempts to improve are likely to fail.

1.5.4 Recruiting Innovators
Several years after the initial interview programme was carried out, I carried out a few more interviews (in 2003) that were related to innovation, they were however a little more general and concerned with Problem Solving. Again there were some very thought provoking comments made during these interviews but one certainly sticks in my mind. The comment was made by the owner and Managing Director of a successful software company based in Scotland. We were discussing the appointment of staff for the company and how to tell if a candidate would be useful, innovative, creative etc. The MD stated that at one interview the

candidate was asked about his hobbies. His reply was that he liked riding his bicycle. The MD was rather unimpressed until the candidate continued that his last trip was across America. He had helped to organise the trip, organise the route etc and had also had to solve many problems on the way across America. It turned out that this was the sort of thing that this candidate liked to do.

The MD was now very impressed and the candidate got the job. The MD stated that he preferred to appoint people that could show that they had the sort of hobby that involved them in new challenges and problem solving. Many of the staff at the company had similar hobbies. They may not be related to software development, one renovated cars and again this did not sound very impressive at the interview until the scale and serious nature of his hobby was revealed.

The MD was of the impression that such people brought new things to the company and that when the company was presented with problems, he was certain that his staff had the qualities necessary to deal with them.

1.6   The Knowledge Associated with Innovation

About three of four years after the initial innovation project was complete and after the results of it had been tested by others in industry, I was asked to study the knowledge associated with Continuous Improvement. This was innovation in other terms and this new objective study allowed a closer and more critical look at innovation to be carried out in one part of a large manufacturing organisation. The method used to study the knowledge was tried and tested and had been used many times on other business projects. The focus of this investigation was to study the knowledge needed in order to know how to carry out Continuous Improvement in an Advanced Manufacturing Cell at BAE Systems in Samlesbury. The work was presented at the British Computer Societies Specialist Group on Artificial Intelligence conference in 2004 and published later in the Journal, Knowledge Based Systems. I do not intend to present the work here but do intend to draw out some of the conclusions and findings from the work because they add to the investigation into innovation being presented.

During the study, 84 separate items of knowledge were identified. The company did have an existing process for Continuous Improvement (CI) or innovation but this was not fully operational and its effect had faded a little due to other business changes. However, the CI Process was acknowledged as the largest item of knowledge on the Knowledge Structure Map (covering 46% of the map) reinforcing the feeling of the importance of process held by managers in business. The second largest knowledge area of the map (38%) was knowing how to identify areas for improvement. This is interesting because the previous work had shown that ideas are the starting place for innovation, yet here there is recognition that there needs to be something worthwhile to have ideas about. Within this area of work, the Advanced Manufacturing Cell, there was a process and a process schedule. These two pieces of knowledge were shown to be in a key supporting position to most of the other knowledge concerning CI. This again supports the idea that innovation is about something and not simply random ideas. People that are going to innovate in business need to know what is going on there.

Based on information provided by the people that were interviewed in connection with this knowledge study, the area with the highest overall risk attached to it was that of knowing how to identify areas for improvement. This is an interesting finding that contrasts the difficulties associated with ideas and innovation with the difficulties of knowing what to improve. The two highest risk areas identified were the knowledge associated with the decomposition of complex tasks into simpler ones and the knowledge associated with the analysis of customer feedback. Each of these knowledge elements plays an important part in innovation and in this case, they have both been identified as being at risk.

Another knowledge item that is in the highest risk bracket is knowing how to identify inefficient actions. On the Knowledge Structure Map, this is closely associated with knowing how to decompose a task into simpler elements and how to identify what areas require improvement, all of which are at high risk. These elements of knowledge together form an interesting component of innovation.
Another of the highest risk items of knowledge to be identified was that of knowing how to maintain motivation. Note that this knowledge is not, how to motivate, but how to maintain motivation over a longer

period. The close link between motivation and innovation is a theme of the whole research initiative and one that cannot be ignored. It is especially relevant because motivation is something that is often needed for the general well being of a business even if the business is not innovating. Although there are a number of strategies that have been shown to work that improve motivation, it is acknowledged that motivation is not a constant state, it can fluctuate wildly.

At the heart of the existing effort to support Continuous Improvement in the manufacturing cell was the knowledge of measurement and analysis of measured data. A section of the Knowledge Structure Map was devoted to process measurement but measurement and the analysis of measured data also featured elsewhere on the map. Whilst measurement was not seen as the highest of risk in terms of the knowledge resource, it was seen as central to continuous improvement.

One of the many findings from the study was that Continuous Improvement or Innovation was not seen as a knowledge generator. Clearly innovation is a knowledge generator, but if the fact is not recognised then there will probably be no attempt made to save and organise the knowledge generated so that it can be reused. It is often true that innovation generates new knowledge and this can add to a company's knowledge resource and allow the company to grow competitively.

One of the other outputs from the work was the construction of a new process for Continuous Improvement based on the knowledge that had been investigated. This process will be looked at later in chapter 3 along with other processes derived from other work.

Only a small section of the project has been discussed here but it should have given a flavour for the different perspective that was taken on innovation following the earlier research based project. Elements from all of this work will be used to help to develop a more comprehensive programme for innovation in the following chapters.

1.7   Discussion from Knowledge Studies

One of the peculiarities of conducting Knowledge Studies in business is that the focus of the investigation is quite firmly, what needs to be known in order to carry out a task or achieve a goal. The results of this and resulting analysis such as knowledge risk assessment can offer considerable benefit to an organisation. However, one thing that such studies often highlight is that whilst staff, people, know how to do things, the things themselves may not actually get done. The factor is considered again in section 4.9 and refers to business culture. The reasons for the things not getting done can be seen as barriers. These could also feature as barriers to innovation.

One of the main culprits of this problem seems to be time management. People often fail to manage their time correctly and to correctly prioritise their work. This is often compounded because other people that interact with them are also poor time managers and the effects of their poor time management also affect the efforts of others to manage their own time.

Leadership can be seen to be another culprit here. The lack of leadership can be seen to prevent projects from getting started properly and then from operating correctly.

Terminology and the lack of a clear understanding about what people are talking about is also a contributing factor that has emerged in these knowledge based discussions.

In section 1.3.1, people noted that risk was the main reason that ideas are not implemented. The discussion here seems to suggest that another significant reason for ideas not getting implemented could be described as inertia. Inertia to new ideas can come from poor time management, poor leadership and misunderstanding and it is likely that there are several other significant contributors to this general idea of inertia.
Each of the issues discussed here come within the business culture arena. This will be discussed in much greater detail in section 4 but it is useful to note that simple business issues such as time management, leadership and terminology can also become barriers to innovation.

2. Innovation

In this chapter I will consider Innovation itself. I won't start off with any standard definitions, helpful though many of them are. Instead I will consider innovation in a conceptual way and try to take a look at what things are part of innovation and why these things help to provide a more complete understanding of what innovation is. Within this, I will try to consider the relationship that the things discussed share with innovation and possibly why innovation is not really innovation without them.

It would be valid to ask whether this approach is any better than providing a simple definition for innovation, working out the easiest ways that the implications from the definition can be implemented and then getting on with it. This same challenge is relevant to many business issues but more so to innovation. The general nature of the challenge is about ownership of problems. Being told what to do and when to do it is fine if it works, it is quicker and probably cheaper than investing time and effort in the problem. But what happens if it doesn't work, or doesn't work as well as we may have liked, or works for a short time then stops working? How are we then to know what to do about it. An Innovation Programme is likely to do all of these things, but in some way, this goes for all business problems.

This is the reason that this work attempts to provide discussion as well as guidance concerning innovation and it is also the reason not to start this chapter with simple definitions for innovation. The reason is that we really need to understand the problem, or in this case, innovation.

2.1   What is Innovation made of?

Early in the innovation research work, around 1998, the idea that Innovation was closely related to Memory, Learning, Knowledge and Intelligence started to emerge. Knowledge was included because the innovator needed to know something about the target of the innovation even though expertise may not be required in all cases. It was also felt that knowing something about innovation could improve things. Intelligence has been mentioned in interviews in particular with sport where the implementation of complex innovation must be matched by enough intelligence to understand the innovation and how to apply it. Intelligence was mentioned in business interviews as a quality of the innovator. Memory was included because of its close link with knowledge and intelligence. Learning is associated with the other three items and in itself is directly associated with innovation because innovation often creates new knowledge. In addition, innovators often need to learn new things in order to complete the details of their innovation.

At a later stage in the early project, creativity became as much a part of an interview as innovation. For some people creativity was the key and innovation was something that supported creativity rather than the other way round.

Probably the final element to be added to the parts of innovation was 'consciousness', although with hindsight, this should have been attention. Attention was discussed as a key part of consciousness but it is probably the most influential element of consciousness within the context of innovation.

The last element to mention from the original work is 'motivation'. Many of those interviewed saw motivation as a critical part of innovation and some even saw motivation as the main thing to be improved in order to be more innovative. Motivation was seen as so special that I will wait until later in this chapter to discuss it. In the mean time, it is worth briefly considering at least some of the other elements, or perhaps the close relations of innovation, before moving on.

2.1.1 Knowledge

In a business environment, there is a great deal of discussion and an equal amount of confusion concerning knowledge. This has got to the stage where some people in the field of KNOWLEDGE Management say that it does not matter what you think knowledge actually is as long as we get on with it. This seems to simply highlight the confusion that would be all to clear if we said that it was not important to know what 'estate' is in order to understand Estate Management. In the case of innovation however, it is easy to be more certain about what we mean by knowledge. Actually, it's the meaning that I would support in any case but not all would agree. However within the context of innovation it is only useful to consider knowledge as something that a person knows. This excludes books, papers, the internet, databases etc. If this was a discussion about knowledge then it would be worth going further with defining it, but it is really a discussion about innovation so simply firmly attaching knowledge to a knower is adequate for these purposes.

Anyone challenging this may say that an innovator does not need to know lots of things because they can look them up in books, the internet etc. However, this simply means that the innovator needs to possess knowledge related to how to look things up, how to know what to look up and how to critically evaluate what is found. It is still the knowledge of the knower that is important for innovation, unless, I suppose, you had a completely automated computer system that produced innovative ideas.

There is certainly (most of the time) a level of knowledge necessary before an innovation could be produced about a specific thing. Even though the odd, completely naïve innovative idea may emerge, it is not possible to base a programme for innovation on these rare cases. Knowledge is important for innovation.

To make a point however, I remember many years ago, my father coming home from work after being held up in his car, at a low bridge that a double decker bus had become wedged under. It was probably in the late 1950s or early 1960s and the story was one I overheard rather than being told. My father was telling how people were out of their cars looking at the bus and other onlookers were also there. Some sort of experts from the bus depot had arrived and were scratching their heads. They had restarted the bus and tried to reverse it, but it was stuck solid. Apparently a young lad went to one of the experts and asked why they did not let down the bus tyres.

Innovation is often associated with experts, although not always. However, it may be useful, as part of a general look at knowledge, to consider expertise in a little more detail.

2.1.2 Expertise

An expert is a knowledgeable specialist in some area. An expert would be expected to know most things about their area of expertise. The term expert then is very closely linked to the possession of considerable knowledge within a specific knowledge domain. The knowledge possessed by an expert may go beyond knowledge within the domain and cover knowledge that would be seen to be background knowledge to the domain knowledge. For instance, if the area of expertise was in wine, then the expert may also know about the use of cork to stop bottles, about the manufacture of certain types of bottles and where bottle manufacture was situated in wine growing regions.

An expert's knowledge comes from involvement in an area rather than simply reading about it or talking to someone about it. Experts will have met a wide variety of situations within a knowledge area and will have generalised and categorised these situations so that they can predict events in novel situations within the same knowledge area. Experts will have made mistakes as they have acquired their expertise. Memory of some of these mistakes will feature strongly in the development of a particular person's expertise. Mistakes are a powerful shaper of expertise. These are the reasons why expertise is so often associated with innovation. An expert would appear to be in a very strong position to innovate, especially when that expert has other background knowledge and other interests.

It is interesting to ask whether an expert is considered to be a wise person. That is, is expertise the same as wisdom? The diagram here shows a pyramidal structure where knowledge is placed above information and wisdom placed above knowledge. I believe that this relative placement of terms does little to assist in their definition. If we consider expertise to equate to knowledge then the structure would place wisdom above that. But what does it mean to place wisdom above expertise? Definitions relate the term expertise to knowledge very strongly. The term wisdom however is connected with the prudent use or making the right use of knowledge. Wisdom is about making judgements. So where does this leave expertise. An expert may be consulted when one requires a decision in a specific knowledge area. A wise person may be consulted when one requires guidance of a more general nature. It is often portrayed that a wise person may not give a direct answer but supply a more cryptic clue as to where the answer may lie. So an expert may be expected to provide an answer from a considerable knowledge reserve. This must involve more than a simple memory of information since it was stated earlier that an expert would generalise and be able to predict situations in novel events related to the knowledge area. This must mean that an expert is also expected to reason and conclude from evidence and knowledge. A wise person on the other hand, with the cryptic answer may also be attempting to help the seeker of the answer to learn a little more about the situation by encouraging them to think along certain lines. A wise person would still require knowledge however. Maybe the knowledge required by a wise person is not so great within any specific field when compared to the expert. However, the wise person may draw on knowledge of many fields to a lesser degree but may be able to use analogical reasoning to see general patterns that apply in many situations. Such generalisation may not be accessible to an expert because they specialise in one knowledge area. It must be noted here that the word generalisation has been used to cover sets of situations within a knowledge area in the case of an expert, but has also been used to cover situations across knowledge domains in the case of a wise person.

A little while ago, whilst I was working on a knowledge related project in a large company, I was jokingly asked a question, in front of others, by the team leader that I was doing the work for. I responded in a cryptic way. He then reported to everyone that I may not be so wise concerning knowledge as I may claim to be. I responded by stating that wisdom is not about providing answers, it is about providing the best questions. That seemed to be sufficient to become the final statement.

Just as it is interesting to consider whether an expert is in the best position to innovate, it is certainly worth considering if a wise person may be in an even better position to innovate.

2.1.2.1 Expert Knowledge Discussion

The discussion that follows is part of an email transcript that took place in 2000 between a colleague in Germany, a colleague in Austria and me. It concerns Expert Level Knowledge and its implications for business and Innovation. It probably really belongs in the previous section but it is so relevant to the current topic that I have included it here.

Von: John (UK)

Expert Knowledge: In our work we have had the misfortune to have to understand the difference between the knowledge that someone knows (person 1) (for example a specific solution to a problem or answer to a question) and that same knowledge given that a second person is an expert. Both people could know the same set of answers to questions but one is an expert (person 2) who knows the answers because he/she understands the domain and the other (person 1) simply knows the answers to those specific questions. How can you define (simply) the two pieces of knowledge so that the difference is clearly visible without making reference to other knowledge? Any suggestions

Von: Jürgen

Dear John, some suggestions to give an answer to your question: the knowledge of person 1 is a form of knowledge which I would call "solution knowledge" - the second form of knowledge (person 2) I would call "proceeding knowledge". Person 1 knows the solution for a problem; this is could be absolutely expert knowledge - but the knowledge of the second person as an expert is a knowledge which proceeds beyond the answer of the question. I m not sure if I understand your problem in the right way -

Von: John (UK)

I think that you do understand the problem and I note your suggestions.
If we take the idea further and say that within a restricted domain, person 1 knows the answer to every question that person 2 (the expert) knows but does not really know why the answer is correct, just that it is.

However, if someone asks either person 1 or person 2 the same question, they will get the same answer and would be unable to say that one person knew more than the other. In this restricted domain, person 1 has learned a large set of answers whilst person 2 has learned the subject in the traditional way and knows the answers because he/she understands the domain. Yet in this limited domain, there is no answer that person 2 can give that person 1 could not also give.

My difficulty is that for person 1, I can make no assumptions about what knowledge this person may have other than his/her knowledge of answers to all my questions. I could however make assumptions about the prior knowledge of person 2 because he would have learned simpler things before he learned the more difficult ones. There is no structure to the learning of person 1 whilst there is a rich structure to the learning of person 2. But in this one domain, they both have the same answers and one could say, the same knowledge?

Am I saying that it is not just the knowledge that is important, but it is how you get it that is really important?

Thanks for the interest:

Von: Ulli

Interesting discussion you started here! In my opinion it's not the result (the "visible" knowledge) which counts /as you said in your last statement/ but the knowledge structure behind it. Students who learn just the questions for an exam may know the answers but if you pose the questions a little bit different they might be unable to answer it because they do not understand the context. Therefore differentiating knowledge (as a result of a learning process) when it is "visible" is impossible - in my opinion. You may need to take into account the whole learning process before to understand the cognitive structure which led to the knowledge shown.

I don't know if this makes sense but we could also talk about that on the phone!

Von: John (UK)

You have got to be right; it seems to be impossible to distinguish the knowledge of person 1 and person 2 unless you ask different questions. This must mean that it is not possible to distinguish understanding unless one can ask a question that person 1 or 2 is known not to have a direct answer to.

There are many new implications now. Does a true expert (person 2) know what he or she does not know, but the person with all of the answers (person 1) cannot know what he or she does not know?

What are the implications of saying that it is not what you know that is important but the way that you acquire the knowledge?

Would someone in business believe this?

Von: Jürgen

Yes really? I think you are right - but the knowledge is as important as the way you got it in the case of the answer does not work. I mean if somebody ask you a question and you give him an answer he will either have a solution for a concrete problem and if the answer solves his problem it is not important if he is an expert no.1 or no.2 - but if the solution doesn't work, the expert no.2 got the better conditions to find out the mistake - I think the philosophical question of the nature of knowledge depends close to the solution -if it works or not - you can't distinguish the different kinds of "knowlegdes" (No.1, No.2) only by testing the solution in reality - otherwise it really doesn't matter what kind of knowledge you got, the true expert (No.2) will be shown in practice, I think - if I m not dazed and confused now

Von: John (UK)

I think that we all agree that it is not possible to separate the knowledge of person 1 and person 2 without further questions that are not questions with immediately known answers. Jurgen is also correct that only person 2 would be able to develop an answer further in the case that it did not work in practice. This is an important point and is related to the point about the need for further questions.

Our discussion has some strong implications for the way that companies see knowledge (and to innovation). They often want lots of (person 1), perhaps because it is cheaper, they have more control over the knowledge or maybe they have simply not thought about it.

Our work here on 'structural knowledge auditing' has highlighted these points within several companies. This discussion has helped a great deal. Thank you.

I have left grammatical errors in place and errors caused because some are using English as a second language, so that the reader can understand that this was an informal discussion about a topic of particular concern (to me at the time). Any suggested phone conversations are obviously not included but there is enough content here to provide both a flavour for the debate and also to show the value of discussion when trying to form ones own opinions. In addition, the reader may agree that the topic is still open and the conclusions drawn from it are provisional.

The final point that I made in the discussion relates to a particular knowledge study in a large organisation concerning safety. There were, in the same department, two types of 'expert'. These were like person 1 and person 2 from the discussion. There was an internal organisational pressure for more of person 1 but as I studied the knowledge structure, it only served to highlight the considerable gap between the knowledge held by the two types of people and I was, at the time, having difficulties in understanding how I was going to report the implications to the managers from the organisation.

2.1.3 Memory

In the early innovation project work, a substantial amount of information about human memory was added. This was done because it was thought that memory is a very relevant part of innovation and that the people charged with promoting innovation itself should know about memory. This (my) belief has not really changed but the information about memory was really aimed at establishing two main features of human memory. These are:

a) Human memory can be excellent at finding information related to a topic and sometimes information where the relationship is not at first clear.
b) Human memory is very leaky and details are often not remembered, they are filled in at the time of recall. In other words, human memory is not always very accurate.

Whilst feature a) can greatly assist the process of innovation and creativity, feature b) can often help to erect barriers to the process elements within innovation.

The benefit of a) can allow a person with a particular set of memories and past experiences to see novel connections between seemingly unrelated events or things. This can be of great assistance to innovation and can even allow the less frequent, large scale, big idea type of innovation to develop.

One of the problems with b) is that it can mean people assessing potentially innovative ideas can misclassify them as examples of things that have been tried before and not worked. If the new idea appears in some way similar to an old idea, then this may be enough for someone that experienced the effects of the old idea to believe that the new idea is just like it when it may only be like it in a very general sense. The new idea could in fact, correct the problems with the old idea so that this time, it will work.

Although this work does not require the detail about human memory that was provided in earlier work, it may still be useful in terms of being thought provoking, to include one or two examples that were cited in that work. These are mainly sourced from a book called "Your Memory, A User's Guide" by Alan Baddeley.

During the Watergate trials in the USA, John Dean gave such detailed accounts of events that the press called him the man with the tape recorder memory. Since many of the events had actually been taped, it became possible to verify the testimony. It turned out that the broad outline of Dean's testimony was indeed accurate but the detail was highly inaccurate. For instance, Dean's own role was presented as more important and central than it actually proved to have been.

It seems that autobiographical memories are reasonably free from error when considering the broad outline of events. However, errors begin to occur once the details of specific events are required.

In one experiment (Elizabeth Loftus), subjects were asked to watch a film of a car crash. All subjects were than asked the same questions about the crash (About how fast were the cars going when they hit each other?) except that the word 'hit' was replaced by one of the words, 'smashed', 'collided', bumped', or 'contacted'. Estimates were higher when the word 'smashed' was used (40.8mph) and lowest when the word 'contacted' was used (31.8mph) with the expected range in between. Furthermore, when subjects were questioned a week later about if there was any broken glass, those subjects who were given the word 'smashed' were consistently more likely to report 'yes' than the others. In fact there was no broken glass.

An example of a leading question that could influence memory, or at least the report from memory, is: instead of asking, Did you see a broken headlight, you ask: Did you see the broken headlight.
Taken from 'Your memory a user Guide' p190

Roger Schanks theory of 'scripts' suggests that we build many generalised representations concerning the things that we encounter in our everyday lives. When we go to work each day or take a trip to the shops, we are unlikely to remember all of the details from each trip. It may become difficult for us to separate memories into individual events. We may know that we usually buy corn flakes and may be able to picture the supermarket shelf and layout of the boxes, but we may not be able to separate one trip from another in terms of these purchases; unless something unusual occurs that is. So if someone says, 'Did you buy corn flakes from the supermarket last Wednesday?' you may answer yes because you usually do, without actually being able to remember the separate incident.
Limitations in our memories are often most revealing when they are compared with other people's recollections or known facts. Human memory seems to be good at storing generalisations of frequently occurring events but missing out much of the detail of any particular event. Detail is often provided from the generalisations. When this is done, memory may become quite inaccurate. (Source from early research project work)

2.1.4 Learning

One of the recommended ways of improving innovation is to help staff to develop, to learn new things or to acquire new knowledge. Learning is part of business development. When staff know more, the organisation knows more, providing staff can express their knowledge. The problem with learning is that many companies see it as something else to proceduralise. Courses are often organised to solve a staff knowledge problem. Then if staff are sent on the course, they are then presumed to have learned the material. In other words, the course, that can easily become part of a process, becomes the substitute for learning. This quotation from Roger C. Schank (a distinguished expert on learning) may help to make the point.

Practice is an important part of learning, not studying. Studying is a complete waste of time. No one ever remembers the stuff they cram into their heads the night before the exam, so why do it? Practice, on the other hand, makes perfect. But, you have to be practicing a skill that you actually want to know how to perform.

The point raised here is interesting and it brings up the issue of wanting to learn or the motivation to learn. This next extract concerns experiments carried out to look at the effect of motivation on learning.

A Swedish psychologist, Lars Goran-Nilsson, gave three groups of students, lists of words to remember. The first group were given no encouragement other than being told that they were taking part in an experiment, The second group were given no encouragement before learning but just before recall were told that there would be a cash prize for every correct word remembered. A third group were told about the cash prize before learning took place.
There was no difference in the learning performance of the three groups.
Subsequent experiments included social pressure as a motivator, but again, there was no difference in learning performance.
Other experiments have shown that the more interested a learner is in a subject, the more will be learned. This effect though, seems to relate to time and effort spent learning.

Whilst learning can be an important addition to innovation, implementing it for the workforce may not be as straightforward as providing several courses for staff to attend. On a more positive note, people are generally good at learning even though individuals often learn best in different ways. The extracts above both make the point that learning is really something that the individual must do and wanting to do it is perhaps the first step.

Towards the end of this chapter, we will consider how it may be possible to help people to have ideas. It can also be true that people often need help to know how to learn. In my many years as a lecturer, I asked several classes of mature students what information they had been given on different learning methods or on the best ways to learn. In most cases, students could not recall being given any help in how to learn. A few had been given help in how to revise for examinations however. If it is generally true that students are never shown how to learn but some are shown how to revise, then this says quite a lot about what we are interested in as a learning community. We would seem to be more interested in the measurement of achievement than in actual learning.

2.1.5 Intelligence

Intelligence was raised in several of the early interviews about innovation, perhaps without any clear definition for it. The implication within the interviews however seemed to link intelligence to the capacity to understand or ever to reason. In fact, the Collins English Dictionary defines intelligence as 'the capacity to understand, the ability to perceive and understand meaning'. This is relevant both from the perspective of innovating and from the perspective of implementing innovation. In each case, there needs to be understanding. When organisations get involved with intelligence they often do so through prescribed Mind Measuring (Psychometric) techniques. IQ testing however, has its critics and it is certainly not the prescription to solve intelligence related problems that many in business are led to believe.

There are other aspects of intelligence, rather than measuring it, that can be relevant to innovation. For instance, it can be informative to see how people make particular sorts of reasoning mistakes. A few examples will be given to clarify this point. These examples are mainly sourced from a book called "Thinking and Reasoning" by Alan Garnham and Jane Oakhill.

People may believe that the lottery numbers 1,2,3,4,5,6 are more unlikely to occur than 9,16,24,28,34,42 because the latter seems to be closer to what actually occurs even though the combination may never have actually occurred.

In one experiment, subjects were asked to form a very quick estimate from the following two computations:
a)   8 x 7 x 6 x 5 x 4 x 3 x 2 x 1
b)   1 x 2 x 3 x 4 x 5 x 6 x 7 x 8
the median estimates from the groups was 2250 for (a) and 512 for (b). In fact the correct answer is 40320 for both.

Two groups of people were asked to estimate the number of words in a 2000 word passage which contained the forms (one group of people for each form):
1.   _ _ _ _ i n g
2.   _ _ _ _ _ n _
The conclusion that there were almost twice as many of the first form than the second is clearly incorrect

A survey of college students who were asked two questions about a health survey:
1. What percentage of men surveyed had one or more heart attacks.
2. What percentage of men surveyed are both over 55 and have had one or more heart attacks.
Results showed that 65% of those asked gave higher estimates for the second question than the first.

In general, the following statements are valid:

- People are predisposed to remember events which are supportive of personal prejudice than events which are not.

- People often exhibit overconfidence in their incorrect judgements, a factor which has been shown in several experiments. Overconfidence is a source of many errors in business judgement.
- Hindsight bias can be shown to occur in decision making. When people are asked to predict the outcome of an event, they may do so with even chances of success. However, when they are told the results in advance they frequently explain that the results were obvious and that they would have predicted them without the prior knowledge.

These examples can show that there are ways of looking at intelligence that can have a very significant influence on innovation. In one respect, helping people to understand typical ways that their reasoning can be erroneous, can help those people to improve. Certainly, a good place to begin improvement is in recognising what is wrong.

2.1.6 Creativity

A great deal of discussion within interviews concerning innovation, was about creativity. People saw creativity associated with the generation of ideas and the whole process of innovation taking this forward to the delivery of a product or service. Not all useful ideas may be classed as creative but creative ideas often involve breaking new ground.

Creativity is sometimes allied with TRIZ, a process that supports the design of new products, particularly in an engineering domain. It may seem odd to associate creativity with a process but there are a number of techniques or processes that are intended to help promote creative thinking. Some of the most popular of these include Brainstorming, Synectics, Lateral Thinking etc. Each of these techniques is a way of helping people to look at problems in different ways and to more completely investigate a problem and its context.

Creativity relates to a person and a creative person may have some specific qualities. Consider this extract:

- Personal style of a creative thinker:
- Openness to new ways of seeing
- Intuition
- Alertness to opportunity
- A liking for complexity as a challenge to find simplicity
- Independence of judgement that questions assumptions
- Willingness to take risks
- Unconventionality of thought that allows odd connections to be made
- Keen attention
- A drive to find pattern and meaning
+ *Plus the motivation and courage to create.*
Frank Barron 1988 Putting creativity to work. In Sternberg (ed) The nature of creativity. pp 76-96 New York. Cambridge University Press.

We are often able to form our own conclusions about creativity but it can help if we notice some interesting facts:

- Archimedes was not the first person to see a bath overflow.
- Newton was not the first to see a falling apple.
- Watt was not the first to see steam pushing the lid off a kettle.

It may be quite easy for us to separate the following statements into examples of creative thinking or not but in each case, what rules are we using.

- Repairing a punctured bicycle tyre.
- Repairing a punctured bicycle tyre on a lonely road without a repair kit, using items found at the location.
- Copying a famous painting exactly.
- Painting a new abstract scene of a type that has never been seen before.

- ➢ Cooking a splendid meal using a novel recipe.
- ➢ Devising a new successful recipe for a complicated dish.
- ➢ Devising a new recipe that turns out to be rather poor.

Creativity is clearly related to innovation. Understanding a little more about creativity may help us to understand more about innovation.

2.1.7 Consciousness (or Attention)

At one time, it was thought that attention was the same thing as consciousness. Attention is the focusing on one stream of sensor information or thought process to the exclusion of other potentially distracting streams. Many of the things we attend to require conscious thought. However, there are some things that we can attend to that do not require our conscious intervention. One example of this may be an experienced driver carrying out the mechanisms of driving without conscious awareness.

There is a great deal of evidence to support the belief that processing goes on at a sub conscious level. Sometimes we put things out of our mind before an answer emerges later. We may also have experienced the phenomenon of having an answer on the 'tip of our tongue'. In this case it is difficult to bring the answer into conscious awareness although the person knows that it is there, somewhere.

Susan Greenfield's book 'Journey to the Centre of the Mind', creates an interesting image of attention as a field of competing spikes of sensory input, all of which are available within our brain. She describes attention as the largest spike that becomes conscious thought. She claims however, that the other spikes are still there in subconscious thought waiting to compete for our conscious attention. This theory can explain why when in a noisy room, paying attention to a local conversation, we can still hear someone else that mentions our name on the other side of the room, and that this can interrupt our thought and successfully compete for conscious attention.

Abraham Maslow in 'Motivation and Personality', looks at attention from a different perspective and one that is highly relevant to any discussion about innovation. In particular he states "It is common place that attending is determined as well by the nature of the individual organism, by the person's interests, motives, prejudices, past experiences and so forth.". This is the basis of understanding that not all attention given by an individual is fresh and new, often it is stereotyped and categorised depending on the nature of the individual outlined above. Maslow states that it can be the persons own mental health (or motivational state) that dictate whether that person will attend to something in an active or passive way. For innovation to succeed we would like individuals to consider each new problem as unique rather than immediately classifying it as something that has been experienced before. From a business perspective this can be challenged. If a person can quickly deal with problems by using his or her experience and classifying problems as examples of previous ones, then that person may very quickly come up with a solution. However, that same person is unlikely to innovate, or find something new, because they only see examples of things that have been met before.

Maslow's view of attention implies that an organisation should first of all create an environment that helps employees to feel comfortable and safe. It should also help them to understand that in some cases their experience can be very valuable to a business but in other situations they may need to take a fresh look at problems. Many of the techniques discussed to support innovation are intended to help people take a fresh look at things; possibly because it is recognised that under normal circumstances people do not do this.

2.1.8 Additional Components

In 2003 additional interviews were carried out concerning innovation in organisations. These interviews looked more particularly at Thinking, Reasoning and Problem Solving. The common feature with the earlier interviews was that initial analysis concentrated on finding the issues that those interviewed thought were most important. The results from this initial analysis of interview notes were as follows:

- a) Motivation
- b) Problem Solving
- c) Thinking
- d) Trust
- e) Creativity

f) Knowledge
g) Leadership
h) Risk

The issues were identified by initially analysing the interview notes to collect statements of the form:

1) Responsibility is an important motivator
2) Collaboration within a supply chain requires trust

The statements were then assigned to a particular category or issue. For instance the first statement above was assigned to the category of motivation and the second to the category of trust. All of the statements were then sent back to each of the people involved with the interviews to find out which statements they agreed with. The analysis reflects the number of statements collected with regard to each issue and also the number that received unanimous agreement of the original interviewees. There were 35 issues or categories identified but of these 4 primary issues, 4 secondary issues and 4 supportive issues were introduced to interviewees. Issues 2, 3 and 5 were primary issues, issue 6 was a secondary issue and issues 1 and 4 were supportive issues. Issues 7 and 8 were identified during interview and analysis and not introduced to interviewees as part of the interview. This means that 12 issues were introduced as part of the interview following earlier meetings, and 23 issues were captured as part of the interview process. However, many of the initial issues feature in the list of most important issues.

It is interesting to see the concept of motivation at the top of a list about Thinking Reasoning and Problem Solving (or Innovation). It is also interesting to see the placement of trust and the two issues introduced during interviews.

There is a great deal more information that can be derived from the notes of each interview but the point to be made here is that we are building a picture of innovation as possibly a fairly simple concept but one that is embedded in a rich and varied set of enablers.

It is worth remembering that the knowledge study of innovation revealed issues related to knowing how to identify what areas actually need improvement. An important set of knowledge related to this task included knowing how to break a task down into simpler steps and knowing how to identify inefficient actions. This is in addition to support for the importance of motivation and recognition of the key role that measurement and analysis can play in an innovation programme.

Section 2.1 has taken a look at innovation by considering what it is made of. No definition for innovation has been attempted but the opinion of a number of senior organisational figures with some responsibility for innovation has been considered. This opinion, supported by more objective studies has shown innovation to be rich and complex even if definitions for it are simple and straightforward. This is reflected in the size of the task of designing, implementing and maintaining an innovative organisation.

2.2   What is Innovation?

This section should be much shorter than the previous one. A good idea would be to get straight to the point by including a set of definitions found on the innovation page of the internet encyclopaedia, Wikipedia (http://en.wikipedia.org/wiki/Innovation).

1) the process of making improvements by introducing something new
2) *the act of introducing something new: something newly introduced* (The American Heritage Dictionary).
3) *the introduction of something new.* (Merriam-Webster Online)
4) a new idea, method or device. (Merriam-Webster Online)
5) the successful exploitation of new ideas (Dept of Trade and Industry, UK).
6) *change that creates a new dimension of performance* Peter Drucker (Hesselbein, 2002)

(In the UK, the DTI's (Department of Trade and Industry) web resource regarding innovation is also a useful place to visit http://www.dti.gov.uk/innovation/index.html)

These sources are useful to consult but an innovation programme for a particular business should be designed for that business and take into account the ways the business operates and the goals that it has.

Forming an approach to innovation in this work has relied on working with people with an organisational responsibility for some form of innovation. Consulting the article in Wikipidia reveals that some scholars have identified several types of innovation including product and process innovation. This precise point cropped up in interviews and meetings and there was general agreement that we are really talking about innovation, any types that one may wish to identify are not relevant to that basic point.

Consulting information about innovation is beneficial in that it allows access to the thought of others on the subject. This is also true of this source of information. It is unlikely that anyone will agree or disagree with the whole thing but hopefully, there will be enough here to help organisations to develop and maintain a successful innovation scheme.

The main point of this section of the work is to consider the thoughts and evidence presented earlier to develop a useful statement regarding innovation that can reside at the heart of an innovation scheme.

2.2.1 Distilling the thoughts on innovation

It would be difficult to disagree with the definitions documented on the Wikipedia web page since they all fit with a general understanding of what innovation is. The problem is that this general understanding is not enough to help to make innovation work. It is not enough for those charged with introducing, managing or developing innovation schemes. The initial statement about innovation itself must somehow embody the complexities of the things that make innovation work, or as discussed earlier, the things that innovation is made of. Unfortunately, making a definition too long and complex, whilst potentially providing accuracy, will no doubt sacrifice usefulness.

There is however, general agreement that innovation is about the idea. Whilst some may argue that even an unsuccessful idea may be innovative, it is not likely to be an organisational goal to produce unsuccessful innovations.

The earlier discussion makes it quite clear that culture, or environment, is a very big factor in innovation. Culture can mean the difference between innovation and no innovation in any particular business. Environment and culture can be difficult to build and maintain and the work is a long term undertaking.

In addition to the generation of ideas, the organisation itself needs to provide backing for them. In some cases, facing significant risk, the organisation may need to be courageous to harvest the fruits of innovation.

The organisation may need to provide help and support for would be innovators in terms of method and opportunity. Techniques such as brainstorming or lateral thinking or more generally, active attention, may need to be explained and revisited periodically.

Knowledge is important within innovation. In one respect, knowledge is applied during the process of creating an idea. However, innovation should also be seen as a knowledge generator and the organisation will need to respond to this by using procedures that ensure new knowledge is added to the organisation knowledge repository.

Motivation is a key enabler of innovation. Motivation is something that can be developed by the individual and it can be supported by the organisation.

Individuals may need to be creative and be able to give the sort of attention that lets them see problems as something new and also be open to solutions that are tailor made for a specific problem.

Intelligence can be a factor both in allowing innovation to be understood and implemented and also from the idea generation perspective.

2.2.2 Innovation at the heart of the Scheme

A statement about innovation should attempt to summarise what innovation is, as the statements at the beginning of section 2.2 do and some of the statements found in section 1.4.1. The statement should also provide a feeling of what is needed for innovation without being so long and complex that it becomes irrelevant for most purposes. It may be useful to try to compile a statement that recognises the central issues of section 2.2 but also involves the distillation of earlier discussion found in 2.2.1. Such a statement could take the form:

> The creation of productive, courageously backed, creative ideas by intelligent, knowledgeable, highly motivated people working in a supportive environment.

This initial effort captures many of the component parts of innovation, seems to include a definition of innovation itself and is brief enough to be useable. It features the partnership between the roles played by the organisation and the individual or team working within the organisation. I think that it is possible to produce something that includes other elements such as attention, trust and method, given that culture is implied within environment and also that is a more memorable statement to become a flagship for an innovation scheme.

However, I do not intend to attempt to produce such a statement because I feel that the raw materials for one are all here and the statement itself is not intended to apply to everyone, everywhere, it is intended to take its place at the heart of a specific scheme.

2.3 The Goals of Innovation?

One of the most compelling justifications for innovation that I have come across was where a large manufacturer was bringing a new product into full production but it was known that the current production levels did not match those needed to finally make a profit on the product. Initial production had been carried out to manufacture several items as demonstrators and to prove design etc. Full production must happen at a much greater efficiency than had so far been achieved. This called for significant innovation in the manufacturing process. This need for innovation could be put a number of ways:

- Innovate or fail
- Innovate to survive
- Innovation is the way business is run   - etc.

In this case there was a pressure to innovate, to think of new ideas, to improve. In this case the goal for innovation was clear.

2.3.1 Does Innovation need Goals?

Do we, the organisation, want to be innovative for no reason at all or is there some reason that we want to be innovative? This question could make more sense if asked in a different way.

This organisation does not want to change at all, should it be innovative?

There would seem to be no point in being innovative if change was not welcome and not needed. If this is true then innovation is most definitely about change. Having a goal for innovation may imply that the organisation knows how it wants to change. Not having a goal but desiring innovation may be to look for any change in any direction or may imply that an organisation wants to change but does not know how it wants to change. These two positions can be stated clearly as:

a)   An intention to move the organisation towards a desired state
b)   An intention to move the organisation in any direction

When considering the wording of these two positions, it may be likely that most people would select position (a) because position (b) seems to imply chaos. However, if the positions were restated as:

a)   An intention to move the organisation towards a pre defined definite goal state
b)   An Intention to improve the organisation but be open to any opportunity

Now maybe statement (b) looks more attractive and possibly this makes statement (a) look somewhat rigid or restrictive. The real situation is not usually as clear cut as this. Organisations or businesses usually exist within a market niche. This means that the sort of innovation they require will take them to a better position within their niche but not move them outside this niche, leaving any desire to diversify to one side for now. So whilst it may be attractive to be, "open to any opportunity", an organisation would normally want to make progress in a particular direction.

The goal for innovation would be to generate ideas that are intended to move the organisation towards its business goals.

There are exceptions to this clear statement. For instance, an organisation may have, for some reason, spare capacity and be in a position to utilise this capacity for profit. It may then consider if it could generate profit from some other activity based perhaps on the knowledge and infrastructure that is already available to it. In such a case, the organisation may look for innovative suggestions as to what new venture it could get involved in that would utilise its spare capacity and capitalise on its existing knowledge and infrastructure resource. This would create a different goal for innovation to the one stated above.

The goal for innovation is to utilise spare capacity and capitalise on existing resources to create a new profitable venture for the organisation.

Clearly other goals are possible and it may be that the goals mentioned would run in parallel.

Within an organisation, maybe at a departmental level, individual managers may set goals for innovation that helps that department to improve the delivery of the specific service that it provides. A large organisation may have many reasons to improve and many specific activities to improve in. When setting goals however, care should be taken with regard to the sets of statements (a) and (b) discussed above. Whilst an organisation may legitimately wish to improve its business within its market niche, it should at least be receptive to other possibilities since these just may become the main business of the future.

The statement about innovation at the start of section 2.3 described a situation where an organisation knew that it needed to change, knew how it wanted to change and knew that new ideas were needed in order to make the necessary changes. Therefore it had a goal for innovation and a justification for resources applied to making innovation within the organisation possible.

2.3.2 Does Innovation cost anything?
To be able to justify resources for innovation implies that innovation itself has a cost. This observation featured strongly in the discussion concerning innovation met earlier in this book. The clearest way that the cost of innovation was discussed was in terms of risk. Risk was also sighted as the reason that many innovative ideas fail to deliver actual change.

Risk is related to the cost of implementing a potentially innovative idea. An idea may have a forecast payback related to it but this needs to be offset against the cost of implementing the idea. If ideas will never be implemented because of cost, then it is difficult to see why the ideas are required in the first place. At some stage someone must assess the idea and the cost in terms of the future of the business. The definition for innovation derived in section 2.2.1 called for courage when considering if ideas should be financed.

Innovation does then have a cost and cost is seen at the implementation stage. However, this is not the only cost of innovation. One company described their innovation award that encouraged new ideas. This became a successful scheme, generating many ideas, a number of which led to successful innovative change. What the company did not look at so closely was the time that it took to evaluate all of the ideas generated as part of the award scheme. Nor did they consider the time that individuals and teams would devote to establishing the details of their idea so that it could be presented for an award. In some cases there were likely to be additional costs related to early stage pre-prototype construction and testing etc. These costs were likely to be significant for a large award scheme but they had never been assessed.

So implementation is not the only cost of innovation. There are costs related to staff time, possibly materials, idea assessment etc. All of these factors may come under the heading of opportunity to innovate. There is a cost associated with creating an opportunity to innovate. An organisation must bear this cost if it is to be an innovative organisation. That does not mean however, that the organisation would not wish to know what this cost was and allow for it in business planning. This may mean never utilising 100% of available staff time or adding a proportional management cost for the management of innovation or adding a small percentage to a materials cost to account for innovation etc.

The cost of innovation or of running a scheme to innovate should take into account the likely cost of this activity. Managers should not believe that innovation can simply be something that is done and does not need accounting for. Managers need to make the necessary allowances, when creating a scheme for innovation, which will allow that scheme to operate and achieve its goals without introducing hidden or unseen costs that may adversely affect the organisation.

2.3.3 Micro goals

An overall organisation goal for innovation was discussed in section 2.3.1. It has been acknowledged that smaller business units within a larger organisation may wish to or be required to set different targets for innovation that are more appropriate to the operations of that business unit.

One organisation set a target for the number of ideas put forward by staff in any one year. The target was assigned to a manager that had responsibility for a specific number of staff. More ideas would be expected from a managed area with 500 staff than a managed area with 50 staff. The advantage with targets like this is that they are easy to manage because it is clear what is required and it is easy to design strategies or systems that will deliver the target. So a target could be:

Three new ideas should be submitted per 100 employees per year.

The problem is that although simple, the target is not necessarily useful. For instance, a business area may generate 2000 ideas per year and none of them may be assessed as worthwhile. This would create a significant overhead cost for innovation without delivering any of the potential benefits.

There may be areas of the business where it is more important that new ideas are generated than other areas of the business. An organisation may pay people to generate new ideas or rather to solve problems for at least part of their time and this will affect what target is reasonable for any specific area. Some staff may be working on intensive production targets and have little spare time to think about alternative ways of doing things. Each of these things would affect the way reasonable targets are established.

However, as the previous example has shown, simply generating ideas may not be what is required and a target may need to be more carefully set. The target could be changed to successful ideas or ideas that are implemented or ideas that save money etc.

Targets may not be enough, as the earlier case shows, reward of some sort may spur on the process of innovation. In many of the interviews conducted, senior managers have stated that financial rewards are not necessarily the best sort of reward to use. Experiments concerning motivation, like the one briefly discussed in section 2.1.4, have shown that financial reward is not necessarily a good motivator. Many organisations find that it is recognition and acknowledgement that is necessary in order to encourage innovation by staff. More will be said about this in section 2.5.

Another possibility is to identify a specific problem that requires an innovative solution and invite staff to participate in the solving of the problem through suggestions etc. This creates a very direct target and everyone can see the results of effort. Although this sounds simple, managers will still need to establish a regular set of targets, based on perceived problems. They will need to create a mechanism that will allow and encourage staff participation and they will need to create a feedback system so that staff can see what was done and who made significant contributions. The advantage with this sort of micro target is that it directly addresses the perceived needs of the business. Perhaps a disadvantage is that it may over focus innovation on things that others have defined and innovation about things or problems that are not identified may not take place.

Where an organisation attempts to target innovation in this way, it is very likely that more than one scheme may be needed and that these may need to run in parallel.

2.4 The Innovators?

Much of the earlier discussion concerning innovation was about the innovators or potential innovators. Comment was made with regard to the sort of person that may be innovative; the sort of person that may be creative and the things that such people may do that demonstrates innovative behaviour. However, only a few statements identified in section 1.4.5 were concerned directly with innovative people and even fewer met with significant agreement.

Section 1.5.4 discussed the case of a particular Managing Director that had a strategy for recruiting people that were likely to be innovators. Although the general opinion of interviewees was that people could learn to improve their capability to be innovative or be creative, it was felt that certain people are more creative than others just as certain people are more athletic than others.

Attention was discussed in section 2.1.7 in terms of the capacity that people have to give attention. Maslow's description of passive and active attention was particularly relevant to innovation. He stated that some people are only able to give the passive sort of attention, the sort that is aimed at classifying experiences rather than attending to them as new incidents. Other people are able to give a more active type of attention and these people are likely to be more creative or innovative than the passive attention givers.

Knowledge and Intelligence have been considered in connection with innovative people. People certainly need to know things in order to be innovative but it has been recognised that a person need not be an expert in a particular area to be capable of producing an innovative idea regarding that area. Creativity is partly being able to make connections between situations and as long as the innovative person has knowledge about certain things, innovation is possible. Knowledge about things that are at least related to the area where innovation is required would be advantageous. It is also important to recognise that whilst there has been comment about the capacity for non experts to innovate, it is quite likely that experts are able to produce innovative ideas. It is really more likely that a person knowledgeable in the area where the innovation is required will produce an innovative idea concerning that area. Maybe the naïve person, relatively speaking, is more likely to produce an idea that is entirely new and almost unthinkable. However, this sort of idea is not likely to come along very often.

The question of intelligence was raised in section 2.1.5 in connection with creating innovation and delivering innovation. It is clear that the potentially innovative person is likely to be of at least average intelligence and intelligence is quite likely to be more directly correlated with innovation.

2.5 Motivation

Many of the people interviewed in connection with this work have claimed that motivation has a significant influence on innovation. It is easy to imagine situations in organisations when people may have good ideas but don't bother to tell anyone about them. They may not put ideas forward because their experience tells them that nothing will ever get done about the idea, or because they know that if they tell the manager he/she just takes the credit for it. They may not put ideas forward because if they suggest something they will just be given yet another job to do or maybe the person with the idea just doesn't see why they should help the organisation when all they want to do is finish work and get away each evening. People that are not motivated may simply not attend to what they are doing and never have any ideas about their work etc, even though they are capable of having good ideas if they felt differently about their situation.

There is little doubt that motivation and innovation are closely linked. For this reason it may be useful to take a brief look at some of the theories concerning motivation and then some of the thoughts that senior managers have about motivation.

2.5.1 Theories of Motivation

This is a very brief look at some of the theories of motivation. The outlines presented do not fully represent the theories and are only intended to provide the reader with an impression of what motivational theories cover.

2.5.1.1   Hierarchy of Needs:

Maslow's hierarchy theory discusses several layers of motivational influences. In essence the elements that are more fundamental motivational influences must be satisfied before elements from the next level in the hierarchy become motivators. For instance, intellectual fulfilment is unlikely to become a motivator if extreme thirst remains an unsatisfied motivator.

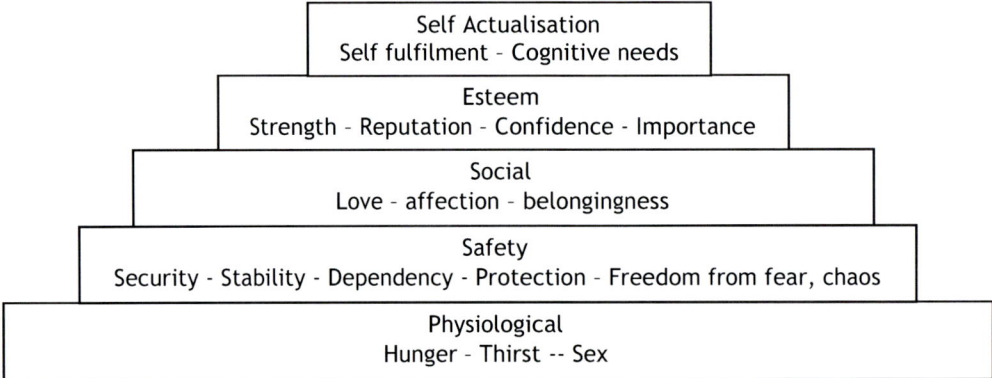

2.5.1.2   Theory X, Theory Y:

Theory X and Theory Y proposed by McGregor, show two opposing beliefs that supervisors can have concerning the motivation of staff in their charge.

Theory X assumes that:
➤ People inherently dislike work.
➤ People must be coerced or controlled to do work to achieve objectives.
➤ People prefer to be directed.

Theory Y assumes that:
➤ People view work as being as natural as play or rest.
➤ People will exercise self direction and control in the achievement of objectives they are committed to.
➤ People learn to accept and seek responsibility.

These two different beliefs will cause supervisors to act in entirely different ways towards their staff.

2.5.1.3   Hygiene Factors Theory:

Herzberg suggested there are motivators that increase a person's job satisfaction. These include achievement, recognition, the work itself, responsibility advancement and growth.
He also suggested the existence of Hygiene Factors that act as de-motivators. These include company policy, supervision, working conditions, interpersonal relations and salary.

Motivators can produce long term positive effects whilst hygiene factors tend to cause only short term changes.

In general, motivators relate to what a person does whilst hygiene factors relate to the situation in which the things are done.

2.5.1.4   Three Needs Theory:
McClelland proposed a motivation theory based on three basic needs.

The need for achievement
➢   Achievement
➢   Personal responsibility
➢   Feedback (to help an individual to measure achievement)
➢   Moderate risk (to avoid excessive risks)

The need for power
➢   Influence
➢   Competitive

The need for affiliation
➢   Acceptance and friendship
➢   Co-operative (co-operating with individuals & groups)

2.5.1.5   Goal Setting Theory:
Providing an individual with specific goals can increase performance. Difficult goals, if accepted, can result in a greater increase in performance than easy goals.

A goal can be defined as an image of a future level of performance that the individual wishes to achieve. Providing specific goals helps an individual to focus on improvement in a specific area. Without this focus, the means to improve can be unclear.

2.5.1.6   Expectance Theory:
Vroom argues that an individual will act in a certain way based on an expectation that an act will be followed by a specific outcome. The individual will be influenced by the attractiveness of that outcome.

Effort, Performance and Attractiveness are influenced in the following way.

Effort   How hard will I have to work to achieve this?
Performance   What is the reward?
Attractiveness   How much do I want this outcome?

2.5.1.7   Equity Theory:
Adams suggests that employees compare their own efforts and resulting outcomes and rewards with other colleagues. If the employee perceives an inequality he/she will act to correct that inequality. This may result in:

➢   Lower productivity
➢   Reduced quality
➢   Increased absenteeism
➢   Resignation

2.5.1.8   Attribution Theory
Attribution Theory has been promoted by Weiner as a key motivational theory, particularly in sport and academia. Attribution theory is a cognitive theory rather than a behavioural theory.

The theory concerns the way people generally attempt to make sense of the world by trying to understand what actions cause which events. An assumption of attribution theory is that people will interpret their environment in a way that helps them to maintain a positive self image. This can mean that when people succeed, they are likely to interpret the success as being a result of their effort. When they fail they are likely to try to blame others for the failure.

The theory states that a person's beliefs about cause and effect will alter their motivation with regard to certain tasks. For instance, if a person believes that success in some task will relate directly to their own effort, they are more likely to increase their effort when approaching the task. In other words, they will give more effort if they attribute success to effort on their part. Equally, if they think they will fail because of some external influence that they do not control, no matter what their effort, they are less likely to put a great deal of effort into the task.

2.5.2 Practical Experiences with Motivation
The following items are taken from comments made by those senior managers etc, taking part in the interview phase of one of the innovation projects. They are not quotations but do reflect what was said by individuals. The comment is separated into topic groups. It is possible that more than one individual made the same observation or comment; no attempt is made here to attribute comment to any particular individual.

2.5.2.1   Does Motivation make a difference?
Across a broad range of sectors, including the business and industrial community, there is broad agreement that staff motivation is important and has a direct effect on performance of staff and therefore the organisation.

➢   Well motivated staff tend to choose to do more.
➢   Poor motivation can cause staff to blame the organisation.

2.5.2.2   Motivators:
➢   Working with the best, the top people. People who are good at their job and confident.
➢   A well established appraisal scheme, taking note of staff needs.
➢   A significant opportunity for training and improvement.
➢   High levels of communication and involvement.
➢   A happy – friendly – supportive working environment.
➢   Good promotion prospects.
➢   Praise when deserved.
➢   Success is a motivator.
➢   Having something to strive for.
➢   Pressure to perform well.
➢   Making people feel responsible for success.
➢   Recognising and acknowledging their difficulties.
➢   Goal setting and establishing personal targets can improve motivation.

2.5.2.3   De-Motivators:
➢   Harmful decisions taken by others that are outside of the individuals control.
➢   Setting too many personal goals, it is better to concentrate on one or two.
➢   Problems from, say home life, can de-motivate during work periods.
➢   The use of unfamiliar terminology.
➢   High levels of stress.
➢   Outside influences preventing staff carrying out their work.
➢   Direct criticism.
➢   Accusative company policies such as automatic sickness reviews regardless of circumstance.
➢   Becoming aware that there is no hope.
➢   Insufficient reward.
➢   Having unreasonably high demands and then having them refused.
➢   Increased accountability and blame.
➢   Changes to working practice.
➢   Not knowing what one is supposed to do.
➢   Not knowing how long employment will last for.
➢   Not knowing what one is responsible for.
➢   Poor motivation can cause staff to blame the organisation.

2.5.2.4 Other factors affecting Motivation:
- ➢ A person's ability to concentrate.
- ➢ IQ may be a factor involved in motivation.
- ➢ Being a public figure.
- ➢ Direct confrontation.
- ➢ Individual ego.
- ➢ Education may be a strong factor influencing motivation. Eg concentration & IQ.

2.5.2.6 Questions:
- ➢ Why does enthusiasm sometimes disappear in a relatively short space of time?
- ➢ Does the motivation of a sales person affect sales?
- ➢ Why does advertising affect sales?
- ➢ How does advertising influence the buyer?

2.5.2.7 Observations:
- ➢ Motivational improvement tends to result from a combination of influences rather than from one factor.
- ➢ It is easier to motivate after failure than after success.
- ➢ Sometimes it helps to know the motivational state of others, particularly when there is a competitive environment in force.
- ➢ People are variable in their nature; some have huge mood swings for instance.
- ➢ Attitudes are contagious.

2.5.2.8 Other Comments:
Motivational programs, that are based mainly or solely on belief, are dangerous. The setting of short term and possibly long term goals where real and measurable achievement is made can be very successful. A feeling that everything is good and that success will surely follow may lead to personal disappointment when things go wrong (as they inevitably do some of the time). If there is no substance to the beliefs about well being and then things go wrong, stress may result. The individual believer may be unaware of the effects of stress because of their positive attitude. They may work long hours and take on more work and responsibility, thus making the stress worse.

2.5.3 Discussing Motivation
During the research phase for one of the innovation projects, an audio (recorded) debate was organised with four people and myself (acting as a chairperson) taking part. The four people included two business owners/managers, one police detective and one senior academic specialising in motivation.

The debate began with a brief review of what people thought motivation meant. When people are asked to do this, it is odd that they refer to definitions in a dictionary etc but if simply asked to talk about it, they use their own experiences. The debate really focused on the relevance of motivation to organisations. The following text will draw out some of the points discussed in the debate.

- It was noted that motivation is not the same as achievement. One person may be highly motivated to achieve something that another person achieves without effort. For some people, even small achievements, by average standards, require considerable motivation.

- The issue of whether staff motivation affects business performance was raised. Staff morale was considered and it was asked if morale is the same as motivation. It was decided that it was not the same but they are linked. It was stated that morale (or being happy at work) is related to motivation. If morale is poor then it is likely that motivation will also be poor, staff will not be motivated to perform well. However, having good or high morale does not necessarily imply high levels of motivation. For instance, a person may be very happy going to work each day and just doing the minimum amount before returning home.

- Although motivation is important to business and can make a difference, it is a foolish manager that designs an organisation that depends on high motivation all of the time. For many companies, for much of the time, there is a great deal of ordinary work going on that only requires normal motivational or work levels.

- Measuring motivation may not be as important as measuring performance. At the end of the day, an organisation is buying performance and not motivation.

- For some work however, such as police patrolling, it can take considerable motivation to continue to do a good job when there is essentially nothing to do other than be there. Some organisations require staff availability rather than constant activity.

- Well motivated and poorly motivated people can be identified in certain circumstances by their response to ideas. Well motivated people may initiate action or identify new approaches where poorly motivated people may look for barriers to new ideas and put forward very general reasons why things should not change.

- Poor motivation or a negative attitude can be infectious as can good motivation or a positive attitude. Unfortunately, it is often the negative attitude that is more infectious than the positive attitude. Attitude and motivation are very closely linked. When trying to motivate a person, it may be good to try to help that person to have a positive attitude. "Attitudes are contagious, is yours worth catching?".

- In many companies the extreme cases requiring high motivation are very different from the daily grind.

- Managers cannot impose motivation on staff but they can create an environment where motivation can flourish (the roots to grow and the wings to fly). Managers can also lead by example to improve motivation and attitude.

- Managers need to take staff ideas seriously, spend time with individuals and discuss their ideas. This can improve motivation but dismissive actions by managers can have a reverse affect.

- It was noted that attitude and motivation can be endemic throughout an organisation. Motivation comes from the top, reinforcing the idea that managers must lead by example. Attitudes can even be detected when telephoning an organisation.

- Self motivation is required where staff spend a lot of time working alone. Self motivation is also useful in general. Self motivation can be a product of the environment that a person works in. This seems to be related to the infectious nature of attitude and motivation. In some cases, a self motivated person could be selfish and not be concerned about an organisation.

- What can managers do to improve the environment for motivation or improve the motivation of individuals? In the short term, for short term goals, bribery may be used. Involvement can be used to improve motivation in the longer term. Showing staff how they are involved in the thing that the company actually produces, even the secretary and the cleaner, can create a better sense of belonging and improve motivation.

- Where an organisation requires 100% motivation from staff, all of the time, this organisation is often looking at a high turnover of staff. It can however, be difficult to continue 100% motivation when ultimately an organisation wins. In other words, it can be difficult to maintain a position at the top.

2.6 Helping People to Have Ideas
Having ideas is not the only part of innovation, nor is it the part that requires the largest investment of resource. However, without ideas, there will be no innovation. Any innovation scheme needs to address the issue of generating ideas. Although it may be unwise to completely rule out the possibility that in the future, machines (computers) will be able to generate ideas, at least in a restricted domain, it remains true that people are the major source of ideas.

An innovation scheme cannot force people to have ideas but it can do many things that help and encourage people to have ideas. Help is associated with method or approach and people may need to have methods explained or be offered idea creation approaches. Encouragement is about the working environment and how a person feels about presenting an idea and what reception he or she is likely to get.

People in business have their own ideas about this part of innovation. Some thoughts about thinking are included below:

> Can you teach people how to think?
> o You can help people to link action to consequence
> Thinking is a proactive thing e.g. thinking ahead
> Failure to think can lead to serious problems
> Some people don't think problems through, thoughts jump about
> More active & deliberate thought in workplace would solve problems
> Thinking about business future is an important task
> Thinking about the whole supply chain is constructive
> Thinking is sometimes imagining possible solutions and scenarios
> Thinking in logical steps is needed in problem solving
> In some organisations, improved thinking in everyone, is beneficial

It is interesting to see that when organisational managers are asked about the elements of innovation, the answers they give and the statements they make are much more closely related to the business process than those made by academic thinkers.

There are a few well known methods that are intended to stimulate the idea generation process. They typically involve free and unrestricted thought that explores new and interesting options without normal practical constraints. I will briefly mention Brainstorming and one or two other approaches before attempting to generalise the help that can be offered to people who wish to generate ideas. The individual options discussed here will not be dealt with in great detail. There is a great deal of information already available about each method. The intention here is to consider them in outline only with the intention of seeing what sort of help people can be offered to stimulate the process of having ideas.

Just before I begin, it is worth looking at the problem associated with misunderstanding which will also be addressed in the next section, in connection with brainstorming. Consider one item from the list above:

> Some people don't think problems through, thoughts jump about

To many, 'thinking problems through' may mean that deeper and more careful thought should be given to problems. However, considering the phrase tagged on the end of this statement 'thoughts jump about' the person originating this statement may have a different idea about what it means. This seems to imply that the originator may believe 'thinking things through' means thinking about the sequences involved with the problem, from start to finish, in a well structured logical order, not just thinking more carefully. Two people with these different beliefs may find it difficult to talk to each other productively about a problem where 'thinking things through' has become the theme.

2.6.1 Brainstorming

I once went to a company that was actively practicing innovation and whose staff had periodic brainstorming meetings where some would argue with those presenting ideas. Others, who mentioned this problem to me, complained about the brainstorming meetings. Really, there was not much wrong in the company, just that it had not been properly explained to staff, what brainstorming was and how a meeting should be conducted. Everyone assumed that everyone else already knew. Assuming that everyone already knows is a mistake often made in organisations. Even if they did already know, they may have a slightly different perspective on the topic than others that are also to take part. Making sure everyone shares a common view of how this particular set of sessions will run, is still a good idea.

The reason for the complaint about the brainstorming sessions was that the point is to get as many ideas as possible recorded, without criticism but encouraging wild thinking, and then at some later stage to try to identify which of the ideas are best, using some pre defined criteria to evaluate them.

During a set of interviews carried out in companies during 2003, the following brief comments were distilled from interview notes and agreed with by everyone taking part.

1) It is important not to reject any ideas in brainstorming meetings
2) All companies should brainstorm occasionally to check direction
3) Brainstorming can weed out unnecessary constraints

Points 1 and 3 emphasise the method, whilst point 2 places brainstorming within a senior management context. Point 3 also suggests unnecessary constraints may creep into business practice over time and these unnecessary constraints could damage the business.

As with other ideas, brainstorming sessions need to be about something. This may be how to solve a production problem, how to design a new component, how to deal with complaints etc but a brainstorming session about everything and nothing may not deliver anything useful.

Criteria to be used to evaluate the considerable number of ideas from brainstorming sessions, should not simply reject anything innovative. An example could be, we reject all ideas that do not fit with company policy. However, looking for ideas that will make the most profit seems to be a reasonable thing to do.

2.6.2 Hats and Rooms
Edward de Bono developed several thinking methods but perhaps the 6 hats method is the most well known. It involves the use of six differently coloured hats that, when worn, constrain the speaker, or thinker, to a specific thinking approach. For instance, the yellow hat, for sunshine, constrains the thinker to only positive and optimistic thoughts whilst the black hat, analogous with a judges black robe, constrains the thinker to negative but logical thoughts that are generally critical.

It is rumoured that Walt Disney had several rooms on which similar constraints were placed. For instance, if a meeting was held in one room, only positive and optimistic views could be expressed. Another room would be reserved for the negative or critical thoughts.

Robert Muller distilled from these ideas, a simpler version of de Bono's six hats method but took great care to give most of the credit to de Bono.

The point about these methods seems to be that they are good at channelling thinking into a supportive and productive style. In a single meeting where one person puts forward points in an optimistic way and another is always critical of every point, the net effect can be to deliver nothing. Where thinking is channelled by adopting these approaches, people are generally working together on both the positive and the more negative aspects, making each more productive.

2.6.3 Out of the Box
The term 'Out of the Box' is used quite a lot in different organisations. It means the thinking opportunities of most people are constrained by their environment and by the rules and procedures that dictate the way they work. In other words, their thoughts are constrained within an invisible box. Thinking outside of the box means to break down or overcome the constraints and have ideas that may be contrary or just different to the things that currently take place.

One example of this is where a person working in a particular production area, on a production problem, was sent out to the market to see if she could find any consumer products that may help with the problem. Needless to say, it was not company policy to do this. In this case, something was found, the problem was solved and a great deal of money was saved.

There is of course, still the problem of how to help people to think 'out of the box'. The term 'lateral thinking' is often used within the context of 'out of the box'. Lateral and vertical thinking were also terms coined by Edward de Bono. Lateral thinking may mean that initially silly ideas are not rejected but projected to see where they may take the thought process.

2.6.4 Six Sigma
Six Sigma is a well defined business process that was originally developed by Motorola to systematically improve processes by eliminating defects. It is not simply a thinking method but the process does generate a real and often targeted need for creative thinking.

There are a number of sources of information about six sigma, including the web site http://www.isixsigma.com. Like any other business process, it has its devotees and its critics and the reader needs to evaluate such processes themselves.

2.6.5 DIY Thinking
The point about the methods listed, and probably about others not listed, is they help to set peoples minds free from the constraints that would otherwise cloud their thoughts and prevent creative thinking. Methods are needed because people do become acclimatised to their working environment over time and become constrained by the processes and procedures that operate within that environment. Process and procedure are necessary for a business so when creative thinking is called for, some additional help may be required as opposed to the expectation that people will simply switch from their normal working environmental constraints to constraint free creative thought when required.

The essence of such thought is really to break free of the constraints that prevent problems being solved and new ventures being designed. Although the cognitive interview may not be directly relevant to creative thinking, it does demonstrate how memories and possibly new ideas can be liberated by taking a multi perspective view of situations. The cognitive interview was designed to help improve eye witness testimony. It does this by encouraging the interviewee to think about the situation from several different perspectives. When the witness has described the event, they may then be asked to describe it again, but this time starting from when the final act took place and considering the things that happened just before that. In other words, the method would help the witness to remember the scene from the end to the beginning. A witness may also be asked, 'what the event would have looked like to a person standing on the other side of the road' etc.

Another way to promote thought is to try to visualise the desired situation and carefully think through all of the details of it. For instance, if a company wished to open a new branch in a new town, visualising the fully operational branch before it has ever been given the go ahead may help. Such visualisation may include imagining how customers would interact with staff on a day to day basis and how one day a customer would come into the office with a complaint and what is that complaint likely to be about. The visualisation could extend to how the branch manager will interact with the local authority or the local Chamber of Commerce or the local sports team etc. Personally, I would encourage this to be done, also, from a knowledge perspective by using Knowledge Structure Mapping to consider what knowledge would be needed in the new branch.

There is no reason why an organisation should not come up with its own method or methods for encouraging creative thinking. It may be useful to consider what sort of things this method should account for.

- ❖ Free people from their daily constraints
- ❖ Channel group thought so that it is additive rather than averaged
- ❖ Think things through rather than write things off
- ❖ Make sure people know what is going on and how to go about things
- ❖ Make sure everyone understands the problem

It can seem odd that we often design a working environment that is functional to the exclusion of the artistic or creative, and then seek to encourage staff to participate in creative thought. The working environment is often unchanging because people like it that way . New ideas are often criticised because they are new and we don't need them. Some managers discourage conversation at the coffee machine and instead choose to measure time at the desk as a measure of productivity.

All of these things make a step change between what normally goes on at work and creative thought. Most employers are more enlightened than the extreme case discussed above but the point to be made is the one about how much of a change is required between normal work and creative thought.

2.7   Idea Management

Please accept my apologies for the term 'idea management'. This is not meant to indicate a specific approach or technique. It is simply intended to indicate that if many ideas are to be generated then there needs to be a managed approach to dealing with them.

The issue is greater than that of taking the idea and eventually using it. The point to make is, a new idea that solves a problem also generates new knowledge. The way a job was done before may now be superseded by a new and better way to do it from now on. It can happen that, when the reason for the new way of doing something has ended, then the new idea is lost. So at some later date, when the need arises again, we start from the original inefficient position.

The new knowledge needs to be recorded and be accessible to those who will at some later time be faced with doing the same work again but on say, a new product. The knowledge may need to be integrated with, or even replace, old knowledge that has turned out to be somehow inappropriate in the face of the new. This is not quite as simple as it sounds if we consider that in a production environment, new approaches may be constantly invented but the new staff that enter the business from an academic world, still get their knowledge from that academic world. In addition, many companies do not have a system for dealing with new knowledge.

In short, it can be helpful to consider the whole process of innovation as a knowledge generator. Then take the next step and discuss what is to be done with the new knowledge. At the same time, we could also ask, what do we do with our existing knowledge, do we recognise its existence and can we find it if we need it?

One way of accounting for the existing knowledge that is particular to an organisation or a process within an organisation is to study the knowledge and record it using mapping techniques. If this is done, when new knowledge is generated, it can be added to the map and associated data as an amendment or as a new branch etc.

Knowledge Structure Mapping records the knowledge that people need to know in order to know how to carry out some activity. Within organisations, such activities are often unique and therefore require specific knowledge. This knowledge is part of what makes that organisation special and unique. Studying it and recording it using a Knowledge Structure Map so that it can be more effectively managed is a good approach to protecting the knowledge and allowing it to be developed when innovation is applied to a knowledge area.

2.8   Knowledge Structure Mapping

Knowledge Structure Mapping (KSM) is mentioned here to show how the knowledge people use to carry out tasks can be formalised and brought into the management framework. It is also intended to allow readers to understand how new knowledge may be recorded and added to the more general knowledge repository.

KSM is a methodology and tool to support the study of any knowledge resource. It considers the knowledge held and applied by practitioners rather than looking at documents, data bases etc. Since it is focused on the human knowledge resource, it uses the way experts acquire knowledge as its structural framework.

The method can be applied to any business area, large or small, and aims to provide decision support information about the knowledge resource for managers within the knowledge area.

2.8.1 The objectives of Knowledge Structure Mapping

The primary aim of Knowledge Structure Mapping (KSM) is to support management by making the knowledge resource visible and bringing it into the mainstream of organisational decision making. In order to achieve this, KSM provides:

➢ A common visualisation of a knowledge resource that facilitates management decision making.
➢ A structured organisational framework for knowledge that promotes knowledge sharing and development.
➢ A learning support option for new and existing staff that can be accessed through an exported html based resource.
➢ Knowledge risk analysis to help identify knowledge that may require urgent management intervention.
➢ Options for Action (OfA) that gives business immediate options to improve and develop the knowledge resource.
➢ KSM promotes an interest in the knowledge resource and an opportunity for staff to contribute directly to it.

2.8.2 Learning Dependency

The map is a diagram of the knowledge resource that shows individual knowledge components (or pieces of knowledge) linked together in a way that reflects how a human expert may learn or acquire the knowledge. It shows the knowledge the expert should already know before being able to fully understand something else. This connectivity is called 'Learning Dependency'. It reflects the way experts build their knowledge on top of other knowledge.

The figure here shows a simple learning dependency diagram that considers part of the knowledge required to play a game of chess. It can be seen that if someone knows how to play chess then they MUST know how a chess board is layed out, what the objectives of chess are and all about chess pieces. Also, if someone did know all about chess pieces then that person must know the value of chess pieces and how chess pieces should move.

Clearly, these latter two knowledge items rely on a prior knowledge of the types of chess pieces.

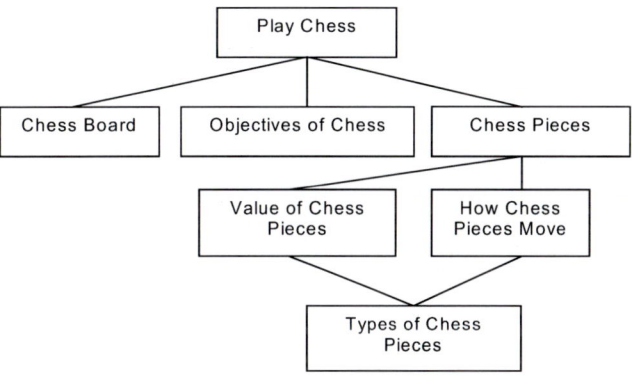

2.8.3 The Information gathered from Experts

Information is gathered within the Knowledge Study Tool, It consists of up to 8 numeric parameters (typically 4) and up to 5 text based parameters (typically 4). The text based parameters are knowledge name, knowledge definition, knowledge summary, a link to more detailed documentation of the knowledge and general notes. The numeric parameters reflect the opinion of each expert interviewed regarding information such as how important this bit of knowledge is, how difficult would it be for the organisation to replace it, when people learn it, is it mainly learned through study or through practice and how many people in this working area have a full understanding of this piece of knowledge. The interviewee is shown sliders to help him or her provide a numeric estimate of the parameter between 0 and 10.

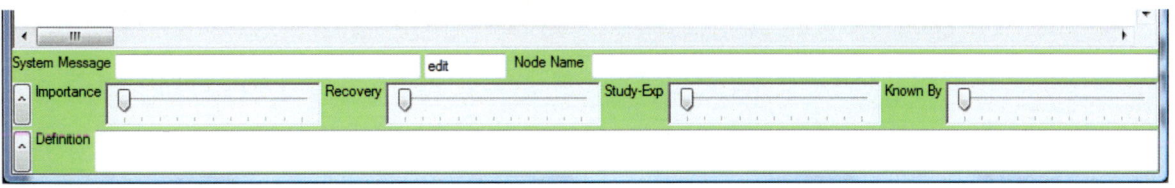

2.8.4 The Analysis

A value for RISK can be computed for each knowledge element based on the data provided by experts and using an appropriate formula. The table shows high risk knowledge elements along with the parameter values that were used in a risk computation. Risk can help managers see where some action may be necessary within the knowledge resource itself and also let them see why such action may be necessary.

Node-Name	Importance	Difficulty	Study-Exp	Well Known	Specialised	Stability	Risk
Derive Knowledge Resource Recommendations	10	9	7	1	8	3	8.42
Improve Knowledge Resource and it's application	9	9	7	1	7	4	7.96
Assess value of a situation.	6	9	9	1	7	3	7.88
Analyse KSM Results	8	9	8	1	8	6	7.88
Construct Knowledge Structure Map	9	8	7	2	9	8	7.46
Conduct KSM Interviews	9	8	7	2	8	8	7.31
Validate a map	7	6	7	1	9	6	7.19
Establish indirect effects	6	9	9	1	6	8	7.15
Identify map structure anomalies	6	6	7	1	9	6	7.00
Elicit parameters	8	6	6	2	8	6	6.85
Map layout	7	7	7	1	5	5	6.85
Use of analysis tools.	8	5	3	2	8	2	6.58
Knowledge context	7	6	7	2	6	6	6.54
Knowledge visualisation	7	5	5	2	8	4	6.54

This table also shows a computed value for risk (0..10) in the right hand column.

The risk profile shows the distribution of risk across the whole knowledge area and reflects the overall risk of a complete part of a knowledge resource.

A range of further analytical options are available including knowledge common to several sub areas and various knowledge probe options.

This is a small sample of the sort of analytical information that is available following a Knowledge Study.

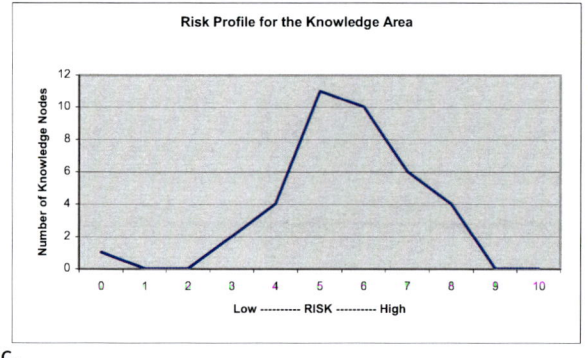

2.8.5 Observations

Observations are derived from the analysis and can include discussion about how knowledge should be developed or protected, which knowledge to take urgent action on, how the results from the knowledge study may affect other business decisions etc.

The Knowledge Study Tool also provides some guidance in the form of automatically derived Options for Action for a whole map or for an individual knowledge node.

Rule Category   :- *Staff development*
Rule Option   :- *Create a community of practice for this knowledge area*
Rule Description :- This involves enabling and positively promoting communication and knowledge sharing amongst experts that may or may not be located near each other. An intranet based system is often used as a core element for a community of practice.

Should be considered for
Knowledge Node :- *Maintenance*

The text above lists just one single example of the many Options for Action automatically generated by a rule based system within the Knowledge Study Tool.

2.8.6 The Software Tools

The main software tool is the Knowledge Study Tool (KST). The KST provides facilities to support elicitation during interviews, analysis, report development, knowledge study and demonstrations. The tool can also be used to extend or modify a map following a review of the project. The Knowledge Study Tool can help with the recording of knowledge by creating files that demonstrate the knowledge to users. It can also export all data about a particular knowledge study as a web based resource allowing anyone with a browser, and access to the documents, to view the resource. This makes a useful focus for the documentation and storage of new knowledge from the innovation process.

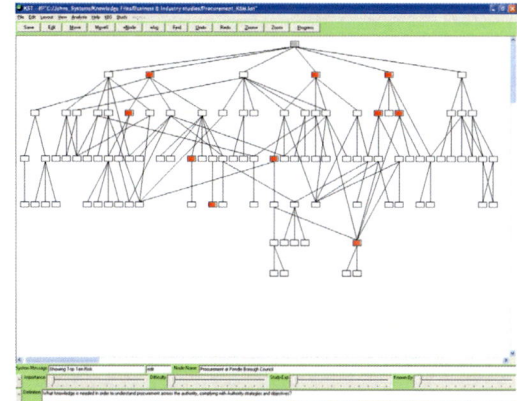

In addition to providing access to all of the data that is collected during a knowledge study, the web resource provides analytical information such as risk assessment and options for action. If staff have been allocated to knowledge elements as either experts or as capable in that area or as having responsibility for that knowledge, then all of this information as well as contact details for the staff are integrated within the web resource. The web resource could also be used as an on line learning aid for staff.

2.8.7 Knowledge Structure Mapping in use

KSM with its detailed methodology can be applied to many knowledge areas and on any scale. For instance, it would be possible to conduct a single project to investigate the knowledge needed in order to run a country and another project on the knowledge needed to repair a puncture in a bicycle tyre. Clearly, the individual knowledge elements on each map would be very different but the maps would probably be about the same size, take a similar amount of time to complete (given the availability of appropriate experts) and would each reveal information about the knowledge area at an appropriate level of granularity.

Under normal circumstances, a large organisation would use KSM for a broad range of knowledge studies but may choose to start with more strategic knowledge areas before concentrating on smaller better defined areas. When a KSM has been used to study a knowledge area, this provides a structured place to store the new knowledge generated through innovation.

2.8.8 Other ways of employing Knowledge Study:

Knowledge Study using a KSM can represent a very effective way to explore the knowledge requirement of various situations meaning that it can be used as a component within the innovation process. KSM can be used as a way of helping people to think about a problem or an idea by focusing on a knowledge perspective. Creative thought can often be released in this way because the focus of attention is shifted away from the normal procedural focus towards a purely knowledge focus.

- **Problem Clarification using a Knowledge Study approach:**

This approach offers a way of working with business experts on a difficult problem. The method allows progress to be made by focusing all attention on the knowledge needed to carry out the task that has become a problem.

- **The exploration of Blue Sky business ideas:**

This approach involves business experts, lead by an expert knowledge analyst, in the exploration of a new innovative business idea or plan. Again, the investigation focuses on the knowledge that will be needed to carry out the proposed activity. This can prepare senior decision makers before plans are carried out or before final planning is fixed.

These two approaches are very similar except that they focus on different issues.

The brief outline discussion contained within section 2.8 is intended to show at least one way knowledge can be handled properly as part of the innovation process and also how knowledge can feature as a target for innovation.

3. Developing a Process for Innovation

I have tried to argue that a prescribed process for innovation seems to fly in the face of innovation. I think that any process for innovation should be designed with the context and the needs of the particular organisation in mind. I also think that the process itself should be subject to innovative improvements as they are identified.

After having stated that, it must be accepted that the design of any process needs to start somewhere and processes for innovation are likely to have quite a lot in common with each other. Also, if there is no current process, then implementing a known process and then being prepared to improve it later is not a bad strategy.

I have possibly almost argued that innovation should not have a prescribed process. However, we have seen the need to create environment, to provide help and method and in general understand what is going on with innovation and how to manage it effectively. All this means is that having a process is likely to ensure that innovation becomes and continues to be, part of the way an organisation works. Managing the process provides something concrete to do and something to improve. It will also be something that delivers results.

3.1 Review of existing Processes

It is possible to find a number of innovation processes and quite a lot of information about such processes. However, I would like to concentrate on two examples. One was the result, or at least part of the result, of a three year project to study innovation and involved many companies. The other was a study within a particular manufacturing company about how they were implementing what they called continuous improvement.

The first project produced a block diagram resulting from many interviews, the analysis of those interviews and involvement of business managers to refine and improve the process. The second resulted from a well structured knowledge study of continuous improvement. The process diagram considered how the knowledge was organised and applied.

These two examples are quite different from each other and were derived in entirely different ways. This makes them an interesting pair of examples to consider when looking at innovation processes again. Initially, I will simply present the processes and consider information that justifies their structure. Any further analysis of them will be left to the end of this chapter (section 3.6).

3.1.1 The P42 Innovation Process

The basic process diagram below is based on the innovation research work. However, there are no real surprises here.

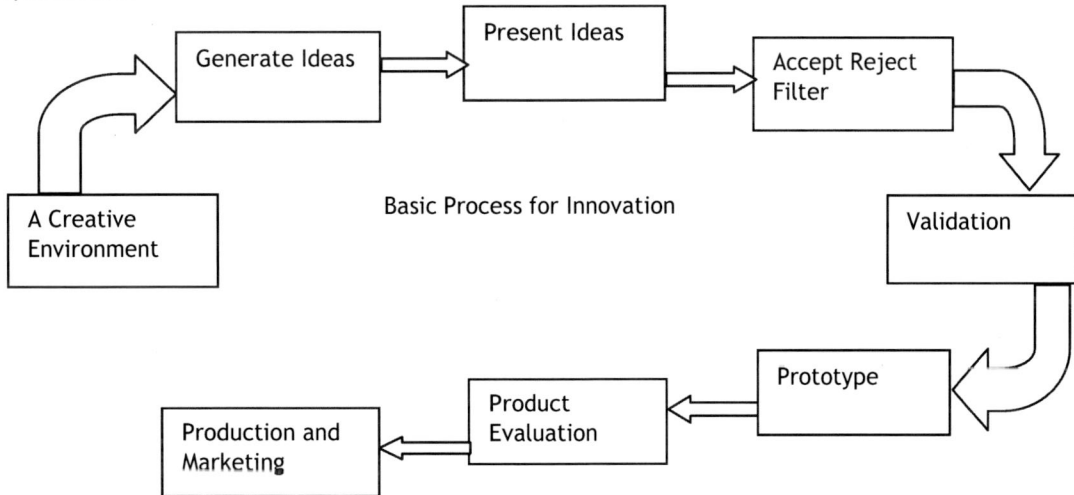

Basic Process for Innovation

Taking each element of the diagram in turn:

Environment: It has been argued that a creative or at least supportive environment is a necessary precursor to the generation of ideas by staff. It may not be seen as a step but without it, the rest of the process is unlikely to happen.

Ideas: It is likely that only a few ideas will lead to beneficial organisational changes. If many such changes are desirable then it is necessary to try to encourage a regular and significant flow of ideas.

Presentation: There needs to be a visible way that people, staff, can pass ideas forward for consideration. This could be a suggestion box, a person responsible or some other method.

Filter: The careful assessment of a large number of ideas can create a considerable resource overhead for a business. An expert, sympathetic and encouraging filter can save a lot of time with idea assessment and can even encourage staff to rethink things and present better ideas.

Validation: Ultimately, ideas will need careful evaluation and risk assessment before additional resources are committed to them. It is important to get the validation process right; otherwise potentially lucrative developments can be lost.

Prototype: Creating a prototype can be expensive, but not as expensive as committing to manufacture. A prototype can uncover unseen difficulties and benefits.

Evaluation: A decision based on the prototype is necessary before finally committing to investment.

Production: A new product or process is implemented and monitored and this individual innovative cycle may be complete.

The process discussed here seems to favour the larger scale idea but it also works for the smaller scale ideas. With smaller scale changes, the risks associated with implementation may be small and things that look good can be tried out. This means that the resources relating to validation and prototyping are almost zero, meaning that the innovation process itself can cope with many more, smaller scale ideas than large scale ones.

3.1.2 The Knowledge Study Project

The first thing to notice about the diagram below is that it is a lot more detailed than the one previously discussed. This is because it was derived from a knowledge study where the knowledge associated with continuous improvement was listed explicitly and many of the separate items of knowledge were themselves investigated. The method is a recursive exploration and provides a lot more detail than would be expected.

The diagram on the right shows the original Knowledge Structure Map contained within a version of the Knowledge Study Tool (a Windows based software tool). This map clearly shows that the knowledge was explored in a hierarchical or recursive way. It is interesting to note that although the Process Diagram was derived from the Knowledge Structure Map, they are completely different and are intended to provide completely different information. It is not appropriate to consider the Knowledge Structure Map in any more detail here, since the topic is innovation. However, presenting the source of this more detailed process diagram for innovation at least provides some context to it and the reader can refer back to section 2.8 for some detail. A paper outlining this work can be found in the

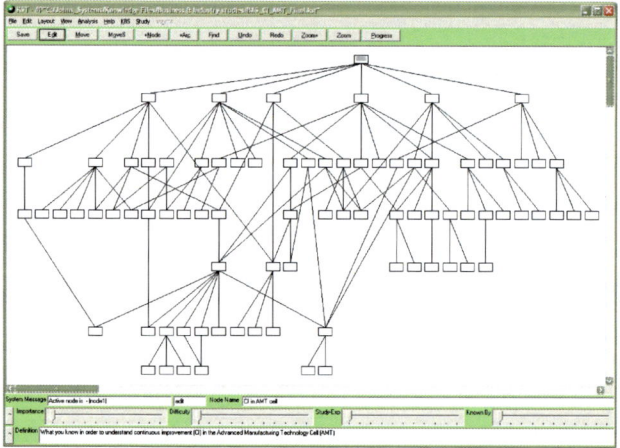

Journal Knowledge Based Systems (Elsevier), 2005. The paper is entitled "Studying Continuous Improvement from a Knowledge Prospective" S Davison, J L Gordon, J A Robinson. The paper was contained in a special issue of the journal from SGAI 2004, Vol 18, numbers 4-5.

I will not list the names of each box and explain each in turn for this example. I will instead discuss the whole process diagram by reference to sections of it and attempt to explain the rationale behind it.

It should be noted that when this work was presented to the company in 2003, the objectives were not the same as those of this work and therefore the conclusions I will draw here are not necessarily the same as the ones drawn at the time of delivery. In fact, this process diagram was not a requirement of the work done, which was knowledge study, it was simply a spin off or an extra and was treated as such. However, it was very well received by the company.

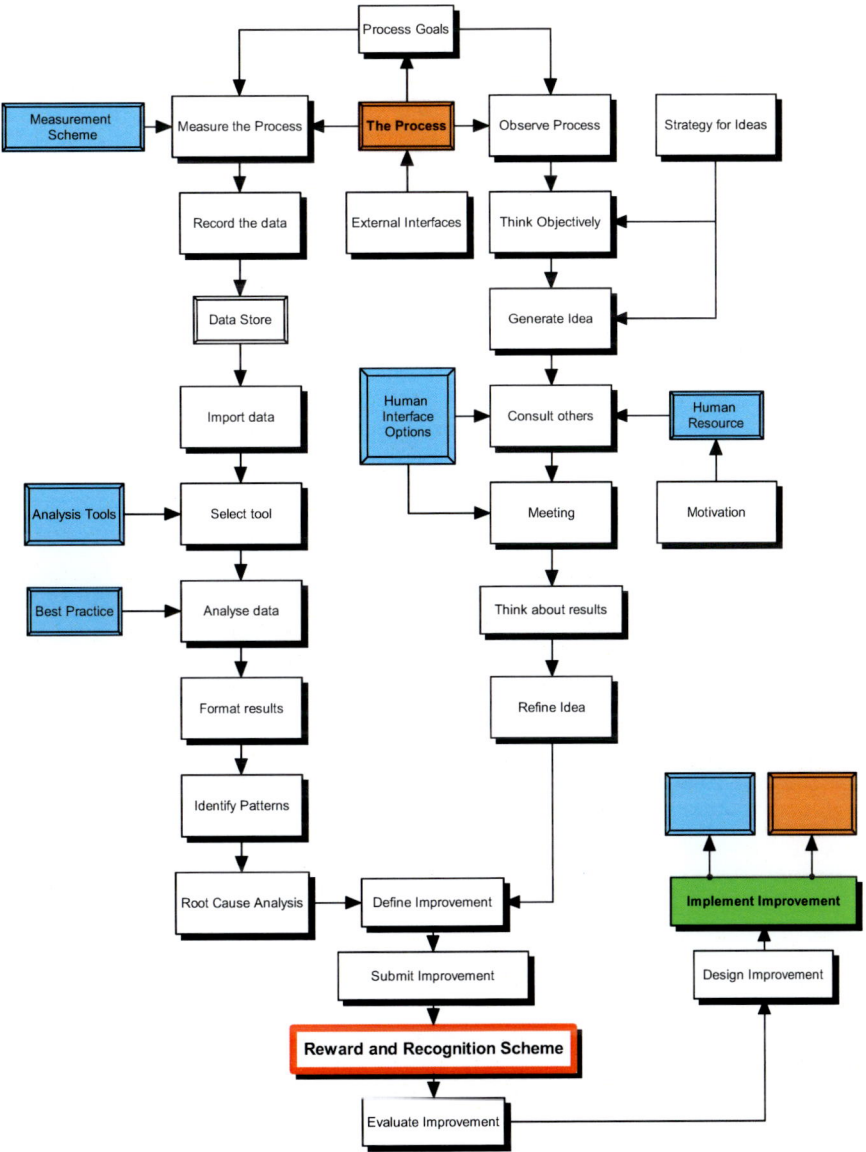

The start and end points of this diagram are more difficult to discern but the process starts at or about the top and finishes near the bottom. It may be noted that the starting point seems to be a box labelled 'process'. In this case, the process refers to the business process that is ultimately the target for innovation. Innovation may apply to more than one business process in an organisation, in such cases, the process means the processes. In this diagram it can be seen that the process is both measured and observed and that these activities, with respect to the process goals, form the place where innovation starts.

'External Interfaces' can be seen to have a considerable influence on the process. This can more easily be seen in terms of customer demand and supplier constraints.

Right at the bottom of the map, the red box labelled 'Reward and Recognition Scheme' acts as a pull for innovation or at least one reason or justification for staff to innovate. It seems then that there is a push at the top, that of external interfaces, and a pull at the bottom, that of some reward or at least the possibility of reward.

After that, the innovation process seems to be shown as two parallel streams. The vertical stream on the left relates to innovation concerned with measurement and analysis whilst the innovation stream on the right relates to the generation and definition of creative ideas based on the thoughts and observations of staff.

It is useful to note that many of the elements discussed earlier in this work are shown in the right hand stream. These include motivation, thinking, support for idea creation etc. The stream on the left is no less important but concentrates on measurement, records, targets, analysis etc. Neither the push at the top, nor the pull at the bottom seem to care which way innovation is created as long as it is created.

The blue boxes are intended to be a tidy way to show how the eventual results of innovation change things. In this case, analysis, best practice, management, human interface or working practice and the human resource in general. The orange boxes show the process itself is evolving as a result of change.

3.2   Identifying the Starting Point

Most of this work has accepted that having an idea is the starting place and a major part of innovation. Creativity is embedded in the act of having an idea but not all ideas need to be creative ones. It is clear that without an idea, there is nowhere for innovation to go, there is nothing to start from.

Having an idea is not an insignificant achievement. As previous research has shown, ideas may come from a range of sources and be sparked off by a variety of events. Having an idea is worthy of some detailed discussion. However, I am not convinced that the idea itself is really the starting point for innovation. If we ponder this situation for a while and maybe decide to try to have an idea, we may expect that at some stage we will come up with an idea. But this is not the case. I admit that someone may appear, occasionally, to have some idea, out of the blue, so to speak, an idea that pops up in an entirely unrelated fashion. The ideas, even the ones out of the blue, are always about something, they have got to be. There needs to be something to have an idea about in order to have an idea in the first place. It is not possible to have an idea about nothing.

In most cases, possibly in all cases, it is a problem, a barrier, a risk, a failure etc that creates the need for an idea. In order to have a useful idea, I need to focus on the issue that the idea is needed for. Once I know what I need to achieve with the idea, there may be a variety of ways that I could go about this including brainstorming, lateral thinking, 6 hats etc, even by not consciously thinking about it, once I know where I am going that is. There is most certainly something that must come before the idea.

Does this observation make any real difference to innovation in any practical sense? It probably does. If an organisation shields people from problems, barriers etc and forces them instead to simply concentrate on what they are doing and get on with it, then those people are not in a position to have ideas relating to the things that are deliberately hidden from them. A management strategy that works in this way may be unconsciously disconnecting a potentially valuable resource from the business development process. There may be good reasons to shield problems from staff, for instance, in a desire to prevent competitors knowing about company weaknesses. However, as pointed out, this can not be done without consequences. The management strategy that operates in this secretive and protective way may be condemning itself to suffering from the problem, barrier or risk for longer than would otherwise be necessary. It may require some innovation to solve this problem for organisations that need to operate secretly yet also wish to elicit the help of all of their expert staff in an attempt to solve problems. However, at least we now know what we need to have an idea about in order to innovate in this area.

Once we realise the starting place for innovation is not the idea but the thing that makes an idea necessary, it becomes useful to consider how a person can interact with the problem, barrier, risk or failure in order to stimulate the idea generating process. A great part of this is the way the problem is attended to. Much of human attention, as Maslow points out (section 2.1.7), is stereotyped attention where we attend simply to classify the problem as an example of something that we already know about. Novel problems need to be given a deeper, honest and more open sort of attention that can really investigate the uniqueness of the problem.

Not all problems, barriers, risks etc are obvious. Some may be invisible and it may involve a creative observation to notice them. Whilst it may be useful to be able to identify the burning issues a company faces and then help to focus the staff resource on these issues, it is also worth remembering that the overall and very general business goals need to be clear. This opens up the possible identification of innovative new ideas to achieve business goals, which are not currently part of operational activity.

3.3   Identifying the end point
Innovation should be a continuous process so attempting to identify an end point for innovation may be futile. However, organisations want innovation for a reason and the reason is derived from the benefits of each successful idea. Innovation really has very many starting places and very many end points. Each starting place is a problem, a barrier, a risk or a failure and each ending point is the successful implementation of a solution to, or improvement of, that problem, barrier, risk or failure. An end point for innovation is probably improvement. In section 3.2.1 a process called 'Continuous Improvement' was discussed. It is very difficult to separate this from innovation other than it seems, even improvements that may not be classed as innovative, are accepted as well as the ones that are. This is probably a more realistic situation for most organisations. It is the improvement that is sought, innovative or not.

One of the implications of this statement is measurement must be part of the process. If it was innovation that was the real goal and if something can be assessed as innovative, then the goal is satisfied. However, if improvement is the goal, then there needs to be some way to establish if things have now improved. More typically, the idea would be evaluated, at least in part, by considering how it can bring improvement and what the likely scale of that improvement will be.

This is part of the risk assessment of implementing a new idea. In its simplest form, this involves weighing the likely cost of implementation against the payback time and then the improved process or increased profit. An idea that has a payback time of five years may be beyond the timescale for the whole project. An idea with a payback time of one month may quickly start delivering increased profit. Of course, there are other considerations to account for when assessing risk. However, the current discussion concerns the end point of innovation and not risk assessment in general.

It is interesting to ask whether the acceptance of 'improvement' as the end point for innovation means that the whole topic is being dealt with incorrectly. Are all of the schemes that help organisations to be innovative, really misguided, should they simply be given help to improve whether it is innovation or not? The definition for innovative, is "ground breaking, pioneering, original etc". But an idea that leads to considerable improvement may not have to be ground breaking or original to be desirable. So maybe innovation is the wrong approach altogether?

Innovation is not the wrong approach, it is simply being used as a catch all term concerning the growth of an organisation. Organisations probably do seek the innovative idea, the idea that helps to establish that particular organisation as a leader and helps to set it above its competitors. However, those same organisations will happily accept improvement, even if this is something that is standard practice elsewhere but introduced new here.

Innovation and improvement will be managed in the same way and the same scheme will cover all. It is however, important to remember this discussion when ideas are being evaluated. The end point for innovation should be a significant consideration when evaluating ideas, not whether the idea is innovative or not.

3.4   Discovering the steps

For any process, it is beneficial to identify steps or stages within the process. These help to ensure that people understand what the process is achieving and also help others to manage the process correctly. With innovation, it can be assumed that once a good idea is thought of, then implementing it is the next step. This can be a very risky thing to do however and it is not recommended for organisations. There will usually be implications involved with the introduction of a new idea. If the idea is a new and quicker way of doing something, then that implies people will stop doing something else or rather stop doing the task the old way. This in itself can have implications.

The inefficiencies of the old task could have been the reason why other things were efficient. For instance, if a new idea is that a particular machine should not be cleaned down after every job but only at the end of the day, this may mean that several more jobs per day may be possible on that one machine. However, after this new idea has been implemented for some time it could turn out that the machine breaks down twice as often as it did before and the reduction of working time makes the whole process more inefficient than it was before. Or, consider a streamlining idea for customer services that means that fewer staff are needed in that area, saving the company money. This could eventually cause so much customer irritation that new business is lost and the company profits suffer in the longer term.

It is important to design and to understand the steps involved with the innovation process so that proper checks and balances can be implemented. It is also important because if something is found to be going wrong with innovation, the process, and its steps, can be improved. If there are no steps then the only option is to innovate or not to innovate.

One of the things the steps or stages of the innovation process must do is to allow or even demand that ideas and the implications of ideas are carefully considered. But the steps or stages must achieve other things as well.

- ❖ The innovation process should allow people to see and understand what the problems are and where good ideas are likely to be well received.
- ❖ The innovation process should encourage people to put forward ideas but with that said; to give careful consideration to ideas they do put forward, to be as sure as they can be that they are good ideas.
- ❖ The innovation process should make the presentation of ideas straightforward and worthwhile.
- ❖ The innovation process should provide a way to evaluate ideas, possibly by ensuring most of the available time is spent on ideas with the greatest potential. Within this, the process should be able to assess both direct risk and any indirect consequences of implementing an idea.
- ❖ The innovation process should be able to back good ideas and if necessary, make resources available to take them further.
- ❖ The innovation process should be able to embed good new ideas into working practice.
- ❖ The innovation process should be able to assess itself.
- ❖ The innovation process should be able to measure performance and know when improvements are made.
- ❖ The innovation process should be able to market itself.

The list above shows things the innovation process should be able to do. Improving such a process may involve identifying other things that the innovation process should do. Many of the items listed can translate easily into steps or stages within the process. Many can be compared directly with or identified in the basic process shown in section 3.1.1. Others may seem completely new, such as the idea of marketing. However, this is related directly to encouraging people to submit ideas. Clearly, if people don't know about a scheme, they are not likely to get involved in it.

The idea that the innovation process should be able to assess itself is an important one. It would be rather odd to introduce a rigid unchanging scheme with the purpose of changing everything else.

3.5   Recognising the Barriers

During the initial research work, many of the barriers or potential barriers to innovation were discussed at the same time as the steps or component parts of innovation. People with experience of trying to implement schemes will often discuss those schemes within the context of the barriers and difficulties they have met along the way. The basic innovation process discussed in section 3.1.1 was developed with the recognition that there were potential barriers throughout the process. The diagram presented earlier will be redrawn here with the addition of the barriers that were identified at the time.

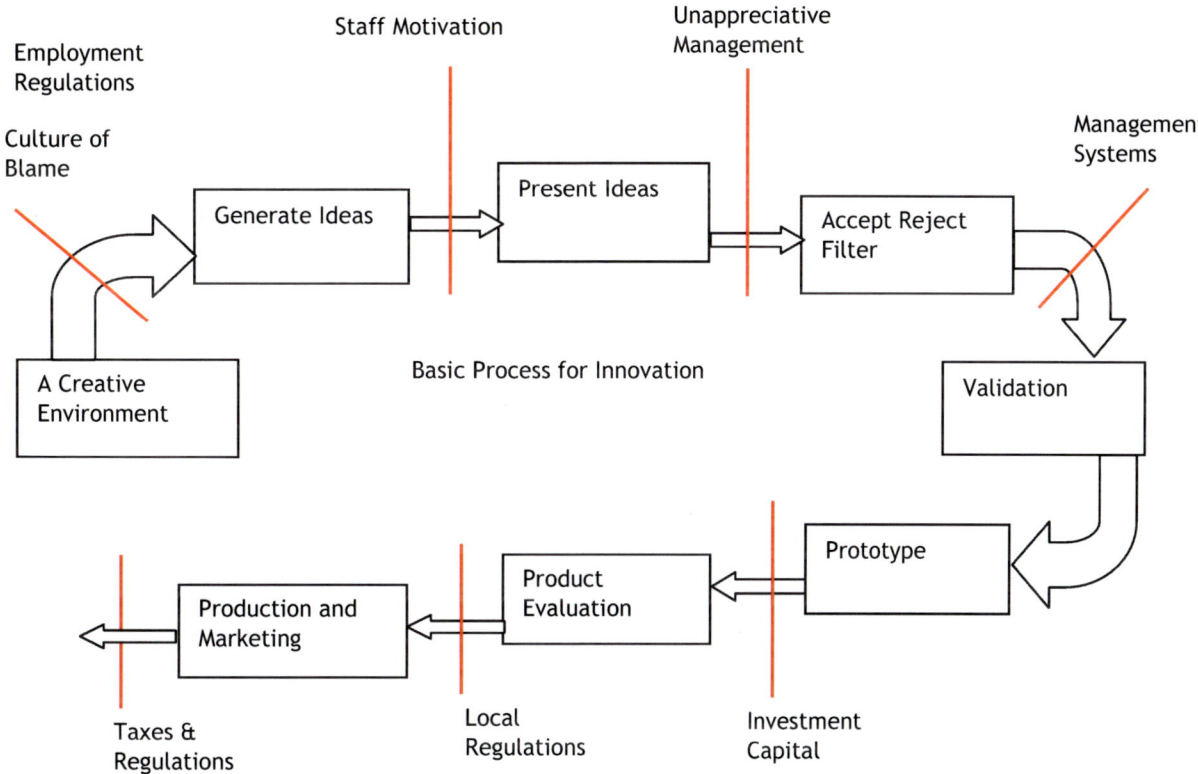

Basic Process for Innovation

Employment Regulations, Local Regulations and Taxes & Regulations all indicate potential barriers that are outside the control of any particular organisation.

A culture of blame will probably suppress idea creation and as shown is likely to stop the whole innovation process. Previous discussion has talked about a supportive environment being a requirement for innovation. A business culture of blame is really the opposite of this and would represent a barrier.

Motivation has been given a lot of emphasis in earlier discussion. Poor staff motivation would represent a barrier to innovation and even if people have ideas, they may never bother to suggest them.

Managers who are unappreciative of, or possibly even hostile to, the efforts of staff with regard to idea submission are likely to stop ideas before they can even get going. This would contribute to a poor environment and is also part of an unsupportive business culture.

In a number of organisations, systems themselves can create a bottleneck so that even good ideas never manage to work their way through the system. This often happens because managers do not make the necessary resources available to implement the system.

In some cases, but not all, an idea may require significant investment. This could even be in the form of a new and different sort of machine. If investment is never available then this will not only affect the ideas that need it but will also have a negative effect on the whole environment for innovation. Organisations may not always be in a position to invest, particularly where the investment is large. However, in such cases, it will be important to make sure that staff fully understand the reasons and maybe they will see this as another problem to solve. How can we achieve what we need to without the need for large investment?

3.5.1 Unique Barriers
The barriers discussed previously are typical of the sort that may be met when introducing and managing a programme for innovation. However, they should not be seen as the only barriers that may prevent the programme form working correctly. Individual organisations may have erected their own unique barriers to innovation or the special circumstances that the organisation works within may introduce new barriers.

The point is that recognising potential barriers to innovation does not simply involve knowing what those barriers might be. It involves actively looking for barriers within any particular organisation. Nor is this something that should be done only when the innovation process is designed, it is something that requires constant attention. Attending to the possibility of unnoticed barriers or new barriers will become an important part of the improvement of the innovation process itself.

Again, understanding the effect of barriers implies measurement. If a barrier is lifted, how will the managers of the innovation programme know this and what difference will it make? Will innovative managers be able to look at a working programme and decide that some part of it is not working as well as it could be and what measures will they use to help them decide?

3.6   A Process for Innovation
The basic process for innovation introduced in section 3.1.1 is a good place to start from. An initial observation could be that the accept reject filter may need to be combined with the validation process to become one element in the process that works better than the two separate ones stated. Some other observations can be made by considering other elements of the discussion and also by considering the process for continuous improvement introduced in section 3.1.2. Some other observations concerning a new process for innovation may be:

> The environment or business culture is not a starting point for innovation it is an enabler for the whole process.
> The starting point for innovation is the reason that an idea is needed. It is a problem, a barrier, a risk or a failure relating to the business process.
> Measurement of the business processes that require innovation should be undertaken and records of measures retained. Changes should be evaluated to find out what difference they make to the process. The process or processes should be monitored through measurement.
> The innovation process itself should be measured and monitored. The innovation process should also be a target for innovative ideas for improvement.
> Staff support should be provided as part of the innovation programme. This should be periodic support to help them with the methods and approaches to idea creation and thinking.

It will now be useful to attempt to design a new process and then consider why each of the elements of the new process has been given its place.

3.6.1 A New Process for Innovation

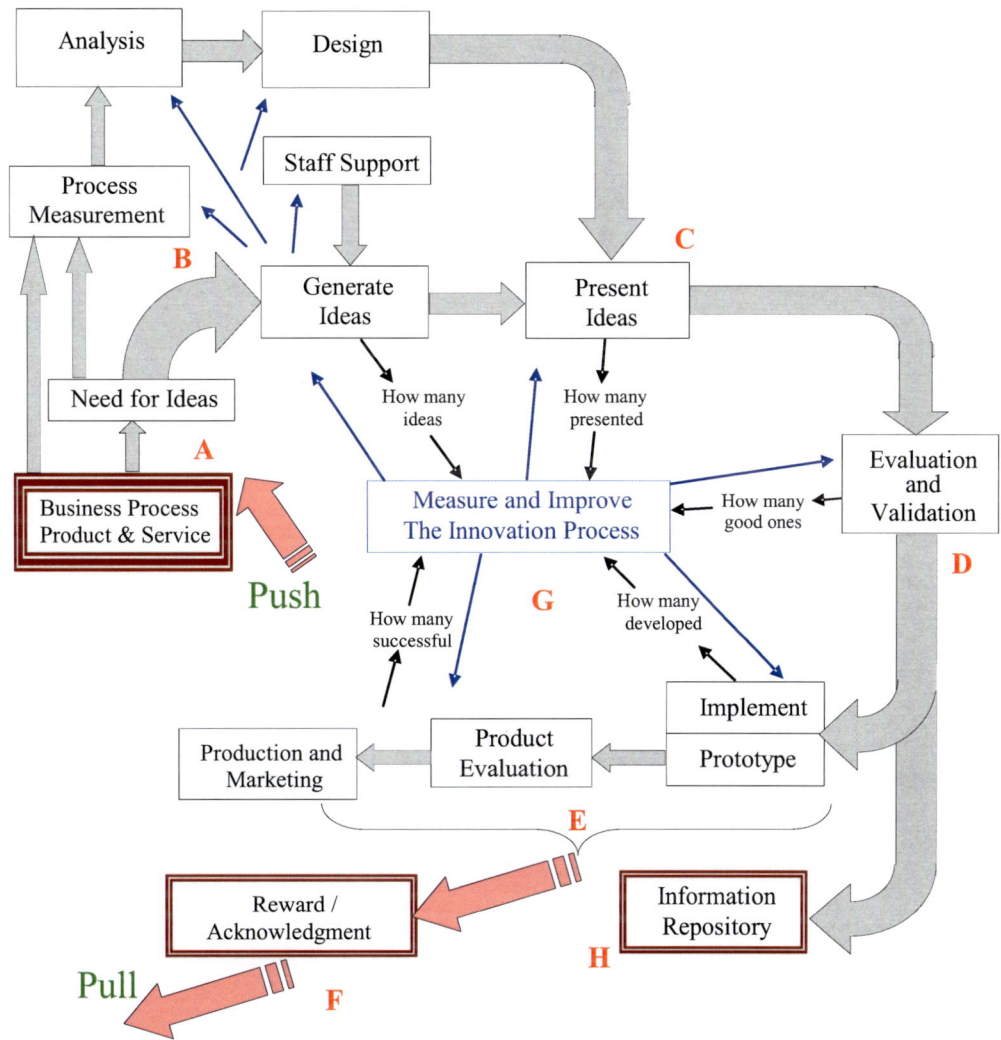

The diagram above attempts to utilise the original and successful ideas about innovation and also address the new and justifiable thoughts concerning the process of innovation. I will examine how this diagram achieves its proposed improvement from the basic process for innovation.

The diagram does now look a little complex but it provides only the briefest of explanation of how the process might work. It is therefore a way of representing and sharing thoughts about the innovation process rather than being the complete process diagram. People wishing to utilise the diagram will necessarily refer to text for clarification. The text will explain what each element of the diagram means. The following explanation provides a brief analysis of the proposed diagram.

A   The innovation process can be seen to start from the business process products and services, just as it should be for a business. The implication here is that people should understand the business process, products and services and their goals. Business process, products and services, provide the push for innovation. The process, products and services are the source of problems, failures risks etc and therefore provide the need for ideas or the reasons for having ideas about the business. This does not simply mean that the business process provides a general need for ideas about how to improve it relating to the process goals; it also provides specific needs relating to problems etc. The business process, products and services are also subject to the requirement to change. Changes may be demanded by regulation, by competition, by technology, by customers and even by business desires and motivation. The business process can be considered as something that includes products and services. For instance, there may be a process for the creation of new products.

B   The innovation process diagram reflects the idea that there may be two paths that can produce innovative ideas. One of these may come from a more analytical foundation relying on careful measurements of the business process and its performance. Ideas from the analysis of data measured from the process may be considered with respect to addressing a specific need or a general business process goal need. The more general process goal relates to improvement, probably ultimately relating to profit. The more analytical stream for ideas may utilise analytical and design processes to address perceived problems but these are also likely to involve human initiative.
The second stream relates to individuals or teams that are involved in or simply observing the business process, noticing how things may be improved. Again these ideas may be of a more general improvement nature or may address specific needs. The innovation process diagram provides deliberate support for staff in terms of helping them with the idea generation process, with thinking, brainstorming etc. The needs for this has been discussed and is briefly related to the probability that the type of thinking necessary for innovative ideas is not the type of thinking necessary to carry out the daily task, or to participate in the business process.

C   Presenting ideas implies a mechanism that can be shown to work. It needs to be something that staff know about and are happy to use. It also needs to be easy to use. However, an organisation may wish to introduce a common format for the presentation of an idea to make the initial assessment process easier.

D   Evaluation and validation of ideas can be a difficult activity to organise. It may need to be able to deal with very many ideas, most of which may be rejected, at least as they currently stand. If ideas are rejected, this should happen quite quickly, taking a small amount of resources for each of many ideas. However, it is important that some sort of feedback is provided for the person or team submitting the idea. This feedback should generally be an encouragement to the individual or team to try again. Where the idea may have merit if it could address some specific issue, such as it will cost too much, then this information should also be fed back to give the proposer the opportunity to make improvements.
Where an idea may have merit, then more resources may be needed to properly consider the idea since the next step may require capital investment. In addition, during this stage, reasons for take up or decision to delay or not use the idea should be justified and fed back to the proposer. It should be possible for a good idea that is not to be adopted to still be considered for some reward or acknowledgement as long as the reasons for not adopting it are made available. Some good ideas that are not adopted by the company may still be able to generate income through intellectual property. The person or team submitting the idea may expect to receive something for income generated in this way.

E   Prototyping, production and marketing needs will depend on the type of idea that is to be implemented. Some idea may simply be changes to the way things are done and may not require any of these things. These ideas may simply be implemented after they have been carefully considered. At the other end of the scale, an idea may involve the manufacture or design of an entirely new product and involve considerable risk and investment. In these cases, this final part of the innovation process will be very important. However, in most cases, prototyping, production and marketing will not be significant or even needed at all.

F   It can be valuable to have some sort of PULL at the end of an innovation process. This may be a scheme to provide reward to the best ideas or it may simply be a way of acknowledging those that have contributed good ideas. In all cases, there needs to be recognition of the part that the people who are submitting ideas are playing in the innovation process and in the success of the organisation.

G   The performance of the innovation process itself should be monitored and subject to improvement. The diagram contains some of the more obvious suggestions as to what could be measured with regard to innovation but there are other things, depending on the way that the process is implemented. This diagrams shows that the number of ideas that are submitted is measured and because there is an attempt to see how many of those come from observation and thought, this means that it will be known how many are coming through the measure and analysis route. As well as knowing how many ideas are classed as useful and how many are rejected, it may be rewarding to obtain other information such as why are ideas rejected. It may become known at a later stage that most ideas are rejected because of cost or that most ideas are rejected because they are naïve. In either case, if this information is known, then managers of the process have the option of doing something about it. Clearly it will be useful to keep a record of what sort of ideas are successful. Are most of them simply procedural changes or are many of them production changes or even product changes.

The diagram shows that the knowledge gained from collecting information about the innovation process and analysing this information, can be used to feed back changes to improve the process. The diagram may only show this in outline but it does diagrammatically show the intention to monitor and improve the innovation process itself.

H   As discussed in section 2.7, it is useful to see the innovation process as a knowledge or information generator. If this is done then each new and successful idea should be stored so that the idea adds to the company information repository and staff using it in the future will benefit from the successful new ideas generated today. The information repository shown in the diagram is a block with one input. This is clearly not how the information repository would look if it were considered separately. It would contain other information that the company uses and generates. It would have an access point to allow staff to gain insight from it and to search it for information relevant to a new task. It may also have a librarian that will organise the information and delete or archive conflicting information that has perhaps been superseded by new approaches or new technology.

This new innovation process diagram provides a good place from which to start to develop a specific organisational scheme. It includes the necessary elements that have been discussed earlier but leaves opportunity to make changes that would suit the specific needs of an organisation. The scheme comes with a built in improvement strategy that could gradually change the general scheme by allowing it to adapt to the specific needs of an organisation over some time.

4. A Culture of Innovation and Improvement

The original title of this chapter was "Creating an Environment for Innovation". However, although much of the discussion within innovation is about environment, this actually means the surroundings and situation as well as atmosphere. Since innovation is really about people, then it is really something about people that needs to be discussed here. The attitude of staff, their personal attributes etc. The new title that involves the business culture is probably more relevant to innovation than a discussion of environment. Getting the title right may help with the subsequent discussion. It may be worth returning to surroundings and setting a little later.

Initially it is important to describe what is meant by a culture of improvement and innovation. It may also be useful to consider the reasons why such a culture may be difficult to achieve or to maintain. Ultimately the purpose is to discuss the ways that a beneficial culture can be implemented and maintained, but it will additionally be useful to consider what potential benefits a business could expect from the effort required to achieve the culture. This part of the discussion will consider ways that overall performance can be measured and its benefits weighed against the cost of implementation and maintenance.

4.1   Defining a Culture for Innovation and Improvement:

A culture is the attitudes and values that inform a society. In a business, a culture would relate to the attitudes and values of the staff. This is likely to mean all of the staff unless the culture is seen as applying to only a particular group or section of the business. It may be difficult to implement a culture in a group that overlaps on a regular basis with other groups that are not expected to share the culture. For instance, it may be of little value attempting to introduce a culture for innovation and improvement in shop floor staff if the managers and supervisors are not expected to share this culture. This is not a general comment about multicultural environments, but a specific point that additional organisational issues will arise if the culture for innovation and improvement is not shared by the group.

The attitudes and values of the people working in the group are the thing that will create the culture. This means that we need to know what attitudes and values we need to promote and after that, how to promote them. The attitudes and values themselves are part of the definition for the culture of innovation and improvement so they need to be clarified first. Just to make a more obvious point clear, values are a set of principles or moral standards that a person holds and attitude is a person's viewpoint concerning an object, issue or organisation. I have deliberately left the word 'moral' within this definition because people's beliefs about right and wrong will have no small effect on their own values and therefore their place within a culture. For instance, do they think that the organisation they work for is really doing harm in the world rather than good?

The first step is to work out more generally what things the culture of innovation and improvement is to deliver and then try to use this to identify a set of values and attitudes that would support it. This is certainly not the time to try to discover how these attitudes and values are to be promoted. That is a difficult enough task to be dealt with separately. So attitudes and values can be identified without the constraint of 'how'.

A culture for innovation and improvement is one where people seek to change things and understand the direction in which changes should point. This means that people need to have at least a view of the big picture for the organisation and understand what their part in delivering this is and of course, how they in turn rely on its successful delivery. In this way, people have a chance to see that improvements made by them can help to ensure their own security in the longer term. If people are to consider making or suggesting changes they must feel secure and confident in themselves. This means that they can suggest things without fear of ridicule and they need to feel their contribution will be valued and their experience and knowledge has worth to the organisation. However, they also need to feel obliged to give due consideration to their own ideas before creating a demand for the time of others by sharing those ideas.

Within a culture of innovation and improvement, people need to know how to see through the mundane. Mundane may apply to regular work that is carried out each day and so can become automatic and done without thought. People need to pause occasionally to think about what they are doing and what they could do. Thinking is easily brushed off as something people do and need not be considered explicitly. However, this is not the case; people often don't think much about things. They can often carry out actions and even form opinions without conscious thought; or rather they may not give the sort of attention needed as discussed in section 2.1.7. This is the point really; problems are not going to be solved or improvements made without conscious thought. One may say that problem solutions are often arrived at unconsciously but the situation is really that the solution can only be used effectively when it is transferred to conscious thought.

A culture of innovation and improvement would be one where people could see the links in activities or processes. That implies they understand that their particular contribution is not necessarily the beginning or end of things but a part of the whole. They should understand that it is the success of the whole that is important to them, their colleagues and the organisation. People in such a culture would not be satisfied in the knowledge their contribution was OK, if the whole failed. Therefore, people would look to make things easier for the people that worked in areas that their work could influence or is influenced by.

People would see ideas for improvement as things that would benefit everyone and not just themselves. If they were to simply seek personal reward from ideas, they may not be too willing to discuss them. People would be happy to acknowledge the originator of an idea and the originator would be willing and happy to acknowledge the contributions to the idea, made by others, in the development of the idea. People would see that ideas were things that could improve security for everyone and would therefore be happy to encourage colleagues as well as develop their own.

People within this culture would need to be good listeners and accept comment in an analytical rather than a critical way. This means they would readily consider suggestions from colleagues working in areas other than their own concerning ways that changes could lead to improvements. They may not be too eager to adopt changes without thought, even from someone in a senior position. However, they would willingly embrace changes where a good case for the change can be made. In parallel with this, each person within the culture would not feel hesitant about making well thought suggestions to others in a sensitive and analytical way. When they make suggestions it would result from considerable contemplation and not immediate un-thought reaction. They may even have discussion with others in order to test an idea out properly where they could see that others possessed information that may be necessary for proper consideration of the idea. People would consider that listening to and proposing ideas was a learning and development process for all parties.

No culture of innovation and improvement could succeed without the capability to visualise and project. Visualisation is a process of creating an internal mental picture of a situation that can be manipulated and tested by the thinker. Being able to share this visualisation with others is not so easy and efforts to do so usually result in others creating similar but different internal models that draw from a separate set of past personal experiences. This need not be so much of a problem as long as those attempting to share such mental imagery understand the difficulties and take steps to minimise misunderstandings. The projection of an image is to be able to move the image forward in time to a situation where things are much better, problems have been solved and efficiency is at a maximum. Once this is done, comparing the difference between two images can lead to the identification of targets for innovation and improvement. It may not be reasonable to expect that all people can acquire this capability equally, it may be enough to ensure that the capability is visible and active within the culture somewhere.

So maybe the culture that is being sought is one where:
   a) People see the bigger picture and seek to make things better because they have a stake in overall success and have confidence in their own ability to make a difference.
   b) People know how to induce conscious thought and attention within themselves and understand how to use this to investigate and challenge.
   c) People see their role as a contribution to many roles and understand that the need is for the success of all rather than any separate component. They seek to understand how separate operations link together to achieve a common goal.
   d) People willingly acknowledge the originator of ideas and happily acknowledge the contribution of others to their original ideas. However, they see ideas as things that benefit everyone and not things that can lead to personal reward.
   e) People are good and active listeners. They are also thoughtful and sensitive proposers.

f) There is a strong capability to visualise and project within the environment and this capability can be utilised effectively.

One additional point that underpins the rest is that people are not easily distracted from the real goals. The most common distraction is where more time and resources are spent trying to find out who rather than what was responsible for a failure and certainly not enough time, relatively, spent on rectification and ensuring lessons are learned. An environment where mistakes lead to punishment should become one where mistakes are a trigger for help, support and possible training. So an additional element in the preferred culture is:

g) People know they will be supported and helped when they make a mistake.

These elements together suggest a culture for innovation and improvement but it was stated earlier that culture related to attitudes and values. To make the definition more useful, it will be necessary to translate the observations into attitudes and values. An argument against this could be that one could never create a common set of attitudes and values that all people could be persuaded to adopt and practice fully. However, this effort is to define a culture without reference to how it could be implemented so the effort should be directed at defining the best possible culture. Any practical constraints can be considered later.

Desired Attitude	Desired Value	Culture Element
A person's viewpoint concerning an object, issue or organisation	A set of principles or moral standards that a person holds	
A desire to see what difference it makes	See things as part of something bigger	(a)
A need to make sure this bit is right	Contributions are very important	(a)
Thinking about things is pleasurable	People have a responsibility to think	(b)
	People should not jump to conclusions	(b)
A willingness to work with partners	Play your part as well as you can	(c)
A desire to help others to achieve the goal	We are all working together	(c)
A willingness to share in good fortune	It is wrong to steal ideas	(d)
It is good to listen to others opinions	All people should practice listening	(e)
Think how others will feel about things	The feelings of others are important	(e)
A thirst to understand things	Learning is beneficial to the whole person	(f)
A desire to guess how things turn out	People should have a distant goal	(f)
A desire to support others in times of need	People should support others	(g)
A willingness to seek help and support	People should be able to rely on others	(g)

This table of attitudes and values is an attempt to turn a general set of requirements into a testable set of items that are aimed at the people who form a cultural group. So if all members of the cultural group of innovation and improvement held all of the stated values and possessed all of the stated attitudes, this would indicate that the desired culture is at least possible within the group. So rather than trying to set the cultural conditions it may be best to attempt to influence attitude and value. There would still be something that would be needed if the attitudes and values were there however. This would be the capability to carry out things suggested earlier such as the capability to visualise and project. It is important to accept a successful culture will require some knowledge as well as attitude and values.

4.2 The barriers to the creation of this culture
A business cannot really dictate the way a member of staff, a person, conducts their own private life. The problem with a work based culture is many of the attitudes and values that are desirable for the work based culture are also attitudes and values that would cross over into private life. It is beyond the scope of this text to discuss aspects of a national culture that are or are not desirable. However, it is within the scope to discuss a desirable business culture. There are several options here:
   a) A business should only employ people who already share the cultural values that the business desires.
   b) A business should try to change the cultural values and attitudes of staff so their entire cultural value and attitude set is one that will be applied by that person within and outside of the business.

c) A business should seek to ensure staff are able to live within and abide by a particular business culture whilst at work and accept that people may change their cultural values and attitudes when not at work.

Each of these options has some merit but they all have difficulties. Option (b) is probably the most contentious and would probably be avoided in the UK at least. Option (a) may fall foul of some employment regulations if investigated at depth. Option (c) is the best of the three but it has a requirement for people to, possibly, have and apply two cultures, a work culture and a private culture. There is not too much relevant literature about people that are expected to have two sets of cultural values and attitudes but the impression is that it is not easily achieved. However, given that this seems to be the best option of the three, (c) should either be attempted or the idea of introducing a culture for innovation and improvement re-examined. There is some limited information available about changing attitude and values but less about how to encourage acquisition of new attitude and values without discarding old ones. It may be possible as well as desirable to allow option (a) to influence recruitment in a way that complies with other restrictions.

Another significant barrier concerns the maintenance of a culture after it has been established. This is particularly relevant where there are external pressures to switch cultural attitude and values back to private ones even over a short time. Also, if belonging to the culture requires effort, motivation will be a significant factor in the maintenance of the culture. In truth, the maintenance of many things such as work on projects and other long term activities is not a simple issue. However, this barrier is an important one to address because its neglect will mean that considerable initial effort may be wasted. I have never been a fan of things such as weekly meetings regardless of whether there is something to discuss or not, but without periodic input it is difficult to see how momentum can be maintained since friction (metaphorically speaking) tends to bring things to a halt. A further difficulty is where a scheme is designed to maintain the activity, in this case, culture, but the scheme itself can suffer neglect and stop. This maintenance problem can be seen with many non business front line activities and sometimes even with critical projects, leading to frenzied activity at the end.

A possibility that the attitudes and values required for the culture of innovation and improvement may conflict with other attitude and value requirements exists. These conflicts may arise from a person's existing attitudes and values but they could also come from other business initiative requirements. It would certainly be unreasonable for a business to require staff to adopt many cultures, depending on which part of the business they were in at the time. If a business can expect its staff to adopt a particular business culture whilst at work and resume their normal culture whilst away from work then the business culture should be as undemanding as possible and there should certainly be no internal conflicts within it.

There are likely to be difficult cases or individuals, as there are with any culture. Such difficult individuals can have an adverse effect on a whole culture, particularly where the cultural group is quite small. The adverse effect can easily be present even though the disrupting individuals are operating within the normal rules and regulations of the business. A disruptive influence may simply be from a source that will not share the common cultural values and attitudes and may also be motivated to persuade others that the desired attitudes and values are wrong. In any democratic environment, this is a situation that simply has to be tolerated and addressed in a persuasive and understanding manner. A belief that every individual in the business can be encouraged to adopt a desired business culture is simply unreasonable. However, the particular problem is that disruptive influences may be greater due to the smaller size of the cultural group.

One final barrier is working out what steps to take in order to set up and maintain a successful business culture for innovation and improvement is certainly not trivial. This is the problem to be addressed next.

4.3   Practical steps in developing a business culture?

The first step must really be to clarify what is required and what the culture is to be like. Section 4.1 identified seven attributes for a culture for innovation and improvement that represent something to aim for. These are intended as a guide rather than a prescriptive recipe and will at least need to be considered within the context of a particular business. The table that follows these attributes attempts to suggest how the culture would translate into human attitudes and values. Again these translations are intended to guide the formation of a culture. Relevant business focused literature seems to conclude by stating that the culture should be introduced across the business without saying how, or listing a set of specific steps to take that are expected to apply in every situation. Neither of these positions is very helpful because the reality is that maintenance can be harder than introduction and apparently similar situations can sometimes be quite different.

It is important to realise that a culture is about people and changes to cultural attitudes and values should be influenced rather than imposed. In addition, it may be that people are to change their attitudes and values at work so the work environment must help them to easily distinguish between the two requirements. A very important point is that a culture is something that persists rather than being placed or reinforced occasionally.

Some of the initial actions may be to:
➢ Re-examine the recruitment policy to see where selection can increase the likelihood of employing staff that already share most if not all of the desirable cultural features. This means knowing what features are desirable and working out how to assess a candidate's position relative to these features. Such actions must not break statutory rules.
➢ Allow staff to regularly see the whole business picture, how sales are doing, what the final product looks like (touch it etc (where possible)), see where their contribution fits, what customers are saying etc. (not just once, regularly).
➢ Start supporting people who make mistakes and encourage them to see themselves as well qualified in designing measures that help prevent repeat mistakes. However, don't hide the consequences of mistakes from them. It may be good to be honest whilst being supportive rather than accusative. The consequence can be linked to the reason to avoid the mistake in future.

One of the suggested requirements for the work environment was that people should be able to easily associate this with something that is separate from their home or leisure environment, particularly if cultural attitudes and values are expected to be different. However, if an environment is static and familiar, this may not encourage people to think deliberately about the things they do in it. One of the requirements for a culture of innovation and improvement is that people should actually think about things and not simply act in a repetitive and stereotypical way. So there may be some things that can be done to the working environment:

➢ Instead of, for example, having the same picture on the wall, change it, not once a week but sometimes once a day or once every two weeks etc. Cleaners usually visit the work place each day and they could change things about regularly (within guidelines) as part of their work.

It may be said that this suggestion is not a good one because people like the familiar and may feel less comfortable if the environment changes. However, maybe people like the familiar because it means they don't have to think about things as much. Thinking is hard and requires effort so it is not surprising that people may wish to avoid it. One could argue that eventually people will become familiar with change. This may be so, but is it not the state that is being sought.

➢ Try to associate the environment with the product or service rather than having a typical office or factory floor environment. Things such as models, pictures, layout etc can influence this.

This action can have two effects, one would be to re-enforce the idea of a work based culture and the other would be to re-enforce the idea of the end product and even the particular place within it. It is simply uncreative to suggest that this is impossible for some industries, for instance, sewage treatment.

➢ Allow people to experience work areas both upstream and downstream of their own work area responsibility. This could be through work rotation or temporary shadowing or even meeting and observation, depending on what is practical in a given situation. 1

This activity will help people to see and understand more of the bigger picture and help people to see how their own work has an impact on the work carried out by others.

➢ Spend at least as much time reporting company successes (and maybe difficulties) as reporting individual achievements. When company successes are reported link these to all staff contributions. Show in a non accusative and supportive way, where business bottlenecks are occurring or where error rates are high or where productivity needs attention and encourage all staff to suggest improvements even if they are not from that work area.

This will again re-enforce the link between the individual and the whole business operation. It is intended to encourage supportive involvement in the whole business so that staff become interested in helping and supporting any business area that needs help in order to improve the whole. This may even mean a shop floor worker making a useful suggestion to an international sales team.

The activities discussed have been aimed at the development of a quite general environmental atmosphere. Even with a cultural framework (rather than specific improvements or innovations) it is probably necessary to take some more direct and deliberate action aimed at helping people to acquire the mental tools necessary to engage fully with the culture. In this case, more direct action is likely to involve periodic information transfer and discussion sessions. This cannot seriously be called training although it could look like this to the uncritical eye.

➢ Organise sessions (meetings and discussions) that aim to explain the culture of innovation and improvement in a human way using the items from the table listed in section 4.1. Attempt to show what things are thought of as good and bad but do not be too dogmatic or dictatorial. People that are expected to adopt cultural attitudes and values should be able to discuss them and even make suggestions and changes if necessary.

This is not an easy thing to do and must be done sensitively if it is not to attract scorn from staff who may feel the company should not tell them what to think. In fact, the sessions should not tell them what to think; rather they should explain a culture that the business is striving to achieve and clearly seeks the help and support of its staff in reaching for this goal. The sessions should also explain why the business wishes to develop this culture and attempt to explain how it will benefit staff.

➢ Organise educational sessions that are aimed at showing people how humans reason and think and how their memory works. This information is readily available in the world of psychology and it can be presented in a way that is interesting and sometimes interactive. These sessions would include other issues such as motivation and thinking etc. Sessions should be periodic and on going not a one day course and then nothing else.

This programme is necessary if a business is serious about developing a successful culture of innovation and improvement. Staff are expected to contribute to innovation and improvement by better thinking and improved attitude and compatible values. Just as people would need support to understand and use a new technology, they would also need support to understand and use their own mind more effectively. Even if this

---

1 Using a phrase such as 'sewage treatment' and then discussing 'upstream and downstream' may cause amusement for some. This is to be encouraged because it shows that certain individuals are making new connections, other than the ones intended.

sort of education is missing from the national education system, it is still needed by a business wishing to grow in the way outlined.

> ➤ Organise periodic business update sessions. Do this in a presentation and discussion environment and don't just rely on the distribution of a business news letter once a quarter.

If staff are really to associate themselves with the success of the whole business then they should be informed about this. They should be made to feel part of the success or concerned about shortcomings. They should be encouraged to correct things if their work area is seen to be a whole business problem and wish to support others if the problem lies outside their direct responsibility. Sessions should seek suggestion and record and pass on good suggestions or ideas to the areas of the business that the suggestion is aimed at. Any ideas generated could even be fed into the innovation process and the source of the idea attributed to the group and the specific meeting.

> ➤ Access to reference sources should be available for occasional query. This facility is necessary when people wish to pursue an idea or see how others address similar problems.

Typically, this resource could be a library but is more likely to be internet access these days. Clearly this resource would need to be supported if necessary by any training that is required. However, this sort of training is usually provided at school.

Finally, it is important to have a group of pioneer staff, probably but not necessarily senior staff, who will promote the attitudes and values stated in the table in section 4.1 by carrying them out in the course of their work. For instance, even senior staff should not be afraid to seek the advice of someone less senior. Junior staff should not comment negatively if a senior person seeks their advice. If a member of the pioneering team makes a mistake, be open about it and concentrate on the solution and avoidance and not on the blame. These staff should never seek to use someone else's mistake as a way of raising their own relative profile within an environment by speaking negatively about the mistake maker. When staff need to make comment about others, they should emphasise their strengths as well as point out problems.

Forming a strong and lasting culture for innovation and improvement will be hard work but it should be worth it. The last thing to do is to consider if it will be worth it and how this claim can be evaluated.

4.4   The anticipated benefits from a culture of innovation and improvement
This question concerning how to achieve the anticipated benefits from a culture of innovation and improvement is really bigger than it looks. It will include how it can be shown that anticipated benefits are realised in practice and also how performance and progress can be monitored. However, first it is best to start by making the claims and stating why each is justified.

Any benefits from a culture change are likely to be gradual and long term rather than specific and spectacular. Although the specific and spectacular could happen, it would be difficult to attribute such an event to the culture. Expectations from a culture of innovation and improvement would quite rightly be more innovation and more rapid improvement overall. There is no need to separate innovation from improvement because it is usually the case that innovation leads to improvement, although it can be argued that improvement can take place without innovation.

It seems that the claims or expectations from the introduction and long term maintenance of a culture for innovation and improvement are easy to make and their value will depend on the values attached to the improvements made. If an initiative to take decisive action to introduce this culture is to be taken then it is important to first consider what things should be measured in order to assess progress and then to take a baseline measurement of these things in order to establish a starting point.

The main difficulty is to decide what to measure. The trouble with this is that if some sensible things are selected, this can then appear to be adequate and enough to influence future decisions. It may not be so easy however to select the best measures or rather not to omit important measures. So a desirable theoretical starting point would be to measure everything possible and to define base line standards for everything, even if the overhead of doing this is high. The aim would be to continue to measure all things for a relatively short time only, whilst using this time to establish which are the most discriminative and useful measures with which to assess the performance of the scheme. Even then, the business should be open to the availability of new and better measures that may appear in the future as a result of new systems or better technology etc. Clearly this theoretical best position may need to be compromised in practice but it is useful to know what to strive for. Creating a base line may take some time but there may be enough time to do this during the planning stages for the cultural change.

The sort of things that are likely to be the most identifiable targets for measurement are those that directly affect business performance. These include production rates (of components and systems), stoppage delays, breakages, bottlenecks, sales, profit etc. Other factors such as sickness days, staff turnover, idea submission and ideas that lead to changes etc are also important. This is a time to be creative and it may be appropriate to measure the office or factory floor temperature and humidity each day to make sure these are not the things that are causing the changes. Creativity in selecting and updating measured parameters to be used to assess business performance is essential because measuring the wrong things or drawing the wrong conclusions from the results can have serious consequences. Things that are not measured can never be shown to influence changes even if in reality the unmeasured element is the key factor.

As the scheme progresses, the aim of measurement will be to assess the effectiveness of the scheme of introducing a culture for innovation and improvement. A positive correlation for this could not be established unless there was a measure of this culture taken and recorded. The easiest measure will be the length of time that the scheme is in place. However, there must also be a set of measures that together can be used to describe the state of the business culture being established. Several easy things will be the number and type of specific events held and how well these are attended and what feedback is received from them. The real measure of the culture however will be the attitudes and values of the staff that are the targets of the cultural development. This could be assessed with a specific well designed questionnaire that should be filled in periodically by all staff involved. The design of such a questionnaire should not be taken lightly since it must be fit for purpose but at the same time practical in terms of staff willingness to engage truthfully (therefore it must be as short as possible). There may be other ways to achieve this cultural measurement and again some creativity is needed allied to an understanding of the particular staff involved. The table from section 4.1 may form a starting point for this task.

Measurement of the environment may be easier but it will still be important to establish which things in a work environment are considered to be good and which things are considered to be bad. For instance, noise, dust, dirt, litter, clutter, space, cold (or heat), smell, broken fittings and fixtures, bad lighting etc could all be considered as elements that affect the working environment. In some work places, certain things that are considered bad, may be unavoidable but others may not be. Once it has been decided what to measure within an environment, actual measurement and monitoring improvement may be much easier. Consultation with staff will still be useful however since an unmeasured element may be one that causes particular concern to staff.

Once a set of metrics has been identified and systems put in place to measure, record, analyse and compare these, it is necessary to consider what improvements or changes would be the minimum needed to make the scheme work correctly and what are reasonable maximum expectations. This exercise is likely to relate to cost and so the business cost of changes in each of the measured parameters should be assessed. For instance, how much does a unit change in production rate cost or make for the business, how much does each absentee day cost etc? If this is to help to establish the success or otherwise of the scheme then it is important to work out how much the scheme is costing to implement.

These points are general business issues and others are more qualified to address these with the care necessary. However, it is interesting to consider that it may not just be (or even be) cost and profit that dictate success or failure. For instance, is it possible to consider a situation where the whole business becomes less profitable but more secure, as a success? Or if the business becomes less profitable but more environmentally friendly, could this be considered a success? There are potentially big issues at stake in changes to business culture. Looking for cultural change that relates solely to the balance book is likely to miss much of the whole picture.

4.5 Facilitating Specific instances of Innovation and Improvement
There are two possible starting points for this discussion. The first is that the discussion starts from a point where a business culture for innovation and improvement already exists and the question becomes one of deciding how to support specific cases within a supportive cultural environment. The second starting point would be to consider how to support specific innovations and improvements in any business environment, even a very negative one. It may be useful to consider what differences could be expected between the two cases. In either case there would need to be information to work from, things that are measured and tests that can be performed. However, there will be some differences between the two requirements for innovation and reasonable expectations from each type. For each of the cases considered, reasonable expectations should be stated and some attempt to justify the claims made. Since all of this chapter up to this point has considered the supportive environment for innovation it may be best to start with a consideration of an innovation against the odds and end up returning to the main theme of the chapter.

4.5.1 Innovation Against the Odds
Is it fair to describe innovation in an environment that is not supportive or culturally enabling, 'against the odds'? If one considers that war is often seen as a breeding ground for innovation in an environment that can hardly be described as one that offers security and stability for the potential innovators, then maybe the claim is wrong. Maybe war is an exception and most innovation takes place in a better environment. Maybe there are few innovators that live insecurely or in poverty or in some other distress. A look back at some highly visible innovation would suggest that war is not an exception and innovation seems to be possible from a broad range of starting places. So maybe the whole of the early part of this chapter which addressed a supportive culture for innovation is misguided.

It is important to note the previous discussion did not set out to list a set of prerequisites for innovation. It simply aimed to describe a culture which would be thought of as providing an environment that could encourage innovation. If the points (a) to (g) from section 4.1 are considered, there are few of these that cannot take place perfectly well in a war environment. So the term 'innovation against the odds' is probably wrong if it is taken to mean that we are considering an environment in which innovation is unlikely to occur. However, from a business perspective, there is seen to be a business need to promote more or better innovation and improvement rather than to allow it to simply take its normal course. It is this perceived need to change the way things may happen spontaneously that has driven the discussion of a culture for innovation and improvement. So the agenda for this whole discussion is driven by a desire to change things whilst not denying that something is likely to happen in any case.

So the starting place for the facilitation of 'innovation against the odds' (recognising that this is not now thought to be the best term to describe the situation) could be to leave things alone regarding innovation and improvement and expect things to simply happen. This simple situation really assumes that innovation and improvement are free to take place but not supported or promoted. However this may not be the case. There may actually be barriers to innovation and improvement that prevent them occurring. In one previous innovation project, several barriers to innovation and improvement were identified by business leaders interviewed during the project. The review of this work shown in section 3.5 shows the barriers were divided into internal and external barriers and are simply listed below without further clarification.

Internal Barriers:
Culture of Blame, Staff Motivation, Unapproachable Management, Management Systems, Inexperience, Investment Capital

External; Barriers:
Employment Regulations, Local Regulations, National Regulations, Taxes

This list is probably not exhaustive but the point is that there are thought to be barriers that can prevent innovation simply happening. This being the case, it is important, even without a culture for innovation and improvement, to identify and remove (or at least reduce) the barriers to innovation to allow any naturally occurring innovation to work. This is not the same as introducing schemes to support or promote innovation; it is simply an act of removing obstacles.

One possible barrier not listed by the managers who were interviewed concerning innovation was free time. This is a sensitive topic in business and avoided by many although not all. At the extreme of the free time issue comes the phrase 'fire fighting'. If people are fully occupied with fighting a raging fire, they may have little or no concern for discussion about how to avoid fires. Such discussion can only come when the fires are out. If the fires, don't go out then such discussion may not take place. The fire fighting metaphor is intended to show that innovation and improvement is not likely if all potential innovators are fully occupied at all times with operational issues. This situation can seem to conflict with a business desire to increase efficiency. Unless staff are fully occupied at all times they are not generating revenue for the business to the maximum of their potential. It is likely that either extreme is undesirable. Staff with a great deal of free time may indeed be inefficient but staff working operationally for 100% of their working time are also likely to be inefficient because they have no time to reflect and consider improvements or changes so the business may eventually stagnate. However, in an environment that is not supportive of innovation, staff may still not choose to use their free time to contemplate innovation and improvement. This is where the culture can make a difference. People should be aware that calculating efficiency in business is often very difficult, not because the method is complex, but because it is not easy to identify all of the parameters that can contribute to the calculation and what the relative merits or weightings of these parameters are. There is also the issue of 'efficient enough' to consider.

The point being made here is a very general one and may appear too obvious. It is that things take time. People should not believe a sudden flash of inspiration leading to a significant innovation or improvement takes only a flash of time. The flash of inspiration may be the result of many hours of thought, contemplation, discussion, experimentation etc. Even those people who appear to enter a new situation and immediately identify a significant improvement are likely to be utilising considerable experience, a practiced awareness of new situations and a capacity to fully attend to a case.

Returning to the topic of 'innovation against the odds', it is important that there is a capability present as well as time. Capability is normally present in business because the staff who work in a business area have been selected and or trained to cope with the demands of that area. They probably possess enough knowledge and experience to do the job required so it is likely that, at least part of the capability is available by default. The remaining question here is to consider whether capability to innovate or improve requires anything additional to knowledge of the work area. Within the present discussion of 'innovation against the odds', it is reasonable to assume that if there is a need for additional capability, it is likely to be present in the environment simply because in the general population, there are some people who innovate even though others do not. So again, if things are left alone, innovation may occur spontaneously as long as the barrier issue has been addressed.

Any other factor regarding 'innovation against the odds', including any requirement for capability to innovate are topics which will be discussed when innovation in a supportive environment is considered. The message from this section seems to be, as long as the staff employed are capable of doing the job and barriers to innovation have been removed including the time issue, then innovation is likely to occur from time to time. The next section addresses the issue of the business requirement to enhance innovation and improvement.

4.6   Innovation in a Supportive Environment
This section will address what is needed in order to innovate and improve in a specific case, assuming the existence of a supportive cultural environment. The requirement for using multiple perspectives and clear visualisation and projection discussed for the cultural requirements would be needed in specific cases of innovation and improvement. These capabilities or qualities would need to be supplemented with a capability in problem solving. This in turn would benefit from a capability to identify problems or areas for improvement and knowledge of strategies that can assist in identification, design and implementation. It may be worth attempting to identify some of the desirable qualities/capabilities/knowledge etc that could support an active and effective innovation and improvement activity.

Within the domain of problem solving would be problem definition and some experience in problem solving and therefore past case memory would be an advantage. In addition, knowledge of several standard problem solving approaches including analogical approaches, trial and error methods and decomposition methods would be useful. These would involve root cause analysis. People may need to know how to identify areas or targets for innovation and improvement. This may involve being able to identify inefficient activities and knowing several strategies that can encourage idea generation. It would also involve being able to assess risk within the situation being considered. A strong knowledge of measurement and analysis would be required including being able to select the most important or discriminatory things to measure.

There is certainly no difficulty in identifying things which can be done to support and promote innovation for specific cases. Maybe a useful way to illustrate the needs of specific innovation and improvement in a supportive culture would be to consider a thought example and at each stage in the example, identify the things which are there to support the act.

4.6.1 A Story about Supported Innovation
This fictitious story involves a mechanic who has recently accepted a new job at a local main car dealer. The job has some supervisory responsibility but is primarily vehicle servicing, a job for which the mechanic has been well trained. He is able to fit in to the new work situation very quickly because it is similar to his previous job but on a larger scale. After a month or so, the new mechanic notices that the mechanics in general spend rather a lot of time simply moving vehicles from place to place.

Why should the mechanic notice this? Maybe because he recognises that the moving process itself is not productive. He must have some experience which tells him that the time spent moving vehicles could be excessive or is at least worth thinking about. He may also have a wish to help the company to become more productive whilst not creating additional work burdens on his colleagues.

He decides he will give the matter some thought.
He has some spare or relaxation time at work. He does not mind doing some thinking at home but it is easier to be in the work place and be able to watch things happening and look for patterns etc. He is not a bad thinker and will often think about other issues which occur in the news or problems that others discuss.
Over a period of time, he decides to keep some records about where vehicles are moved from and to, how long each operation takes, what the reason for the move actually was and a few other things. All the time he is still thinking about the problem and when he gets the chance he asks friends who work in similar jobs in other companies about their situation concerning vehicle movements.

The mechanic is clearly interested and well motivated. He needs to do some analogical reasoning with the present situation, past experience and the information gained from friends. He needs to be able to analyse the data that he collects and recognise which parts of the data are the most important parts in terms of identifying and defining any problem which may or may not exist.

After some time, he notices many of the individual movements are carried out to move things out of the way so that other necessary movements can take place. He has been able to identify a restricted set of movement categories and actual movements which take place regularly. By recording these he has been able to see what takes longest, what categories are most time consuming etc. His feeling now after this contemplation is that things could be improved but he does not know how. He sets to work on the problem.

Clearly the mechanic needs to know the objective of an improvement and be able to work out how to implement it or even assess if improvement is possible. In addition, he needs to know about the risks attached. Will changes make the work environment more dangerous or risk more damage. Risk concerning cost is also something he will need to consider. The cost of a change for a very small saving of time and effort may make the change uneconomic. He may ask for meetings with other people and use techniques such as brainstorming etc.

Following some detailed thought, the mechanic works out that some fairly simple changes to procedure and practice could lead to savings of about 16 working hours per week at hardly any cost to the company. However, a more significant move of one of the main vehicle ramps would lead to over 40 hours per week of time savings or equivalent to one extra mechanic and an associated increase in productivity and hence profit. This more significant improvement however, comes at a cost. A regional company will move the ramp but the cost is significant and the process of moving would cause the loss of two working days for the whole workshop.

The mechanic has used many skills to design a problem solution, to elicit the input of others, cost the changes and assess the risks involved.

The scheme or proposal is now ready for consideration by the management team who will be supportive and positive about the suggestion. They would not have asked him why he was not working when he was contemplating the initial idea because they would have trusted that he was doing something worthwhile. The mechanic was happy about being seen to spend time on this idea because he knew that even if it got nowhere, he would not have been accused of wasting time or anything else.
In the end, the two parts of the idea were implemented and some of the savings passed on to all staff as an initial bonus and then a small salary increase. The company increased its profit margin slightly and better still; the turnover time for each customer vehicle service was improved.

The story may lead others to think of more things which could have been brought to bear on this specific case of innovation and improvement. However it should be clear the environment that both allowed and encouraged the new mechanic to undertake the exercise would have played a significant part. Even if there were no barriers, the mechanic may not have bothered working things out even if he recognised the potential for improvement. Once he recognised there could be 40 hours of savings made by one act, he may then have chosen to hide the work because he could not be sure that the company would not respond by sacking one mechanic instead of increasing turnover.

The story itself is a useful way to help people to see how things can work and what things may be needed and how they could be implemented in a particular environment. Stories like this can become a magnet which attracts input from other people whereas a cold definition of a problem may leave others spending all of their effort trying to work out what is meant rather than what they would do.

4.7   The Environment
During the previous discussion about the business culture, the actual working environment, the surroundings etc, has been mentioned. It will be useful now to bring these together and then consider what changes to the actual environment can be made to support innovation.

It was noted, if an organisation is attempting to maintain a business culture that may be different from the normal cultural environment of its staff, then the staff need to feel they are in a different environment when they are at work and this environment should feel like a work environment. Making people feel 'at home' is probably not a good idea. Clearly this does not mean the business environment needs to be poor or dirty etc, in fact it may even be better than the environment people are used to elsewhere.

Creating an environment that changes periodically, may be useful to help people to notice things more. Changes could be part of, say the cleaning process but they should not be done too predictably such as every Friday etc. Simple changes such as moving the furniture in a rest area or changing the pictures on the wall or even moving the location of the waste bins may be useful, although the latter may cause disproportionate reaction.

It was mentioned that the environment should look like work so having work based pictures, models and products in it may be useful.

It was mentioned that staff would benefit from appreciating the work of others that may be further up or downstream in the product or service process. Items from these other sections, supplier and customer sections, may find useful places within a particular department.

A notice board with up to date organisational information on it may be valuable such as copies of the most recent letters of thanks or support received from customers and production or sales figures etc. If things are not so good at present, then a summary of the reasons for the problems may even spark innovative ideas.

Supporting thinking by having an area where staff can go to find help and even the weekly puzzle could be useful (see next section). Leaflets on brainstorming or explanations of lateral thinking etc could be found easily by staff wishing to innovate. A 'Thinking Station' like this would need to be regularly maintained. It could even be the place where ideas are submitted.

This is just a sample of the sort of things that an organisation could consider doing to the working environment to promote innovation. However, it is always good practice to measure, because changes may not always work the way they are intended to.

4.8   A Thinking Station

This section describes an idea for the deployment and maintenance of a 'Thinking Station'. This is simply an idea to provide a flavour for the sort of thing which could be done. Of course, in any specific organisation, experienced managers will have to consider this idea within the context of what they know about their staff. However, just because staff may have reacted negatively to other things should not prevent this one from being tested.

The aim of the 'Thinking Station' is to create a changing resource that will be placed in a business area where many of the staff either pass or spend time. The aim of the 'Thinking Station' will be to encourage staff to think more and think more effectively and in this way become generally more innovative and creative in the work environment and hopefully in their own lives away from work.

The 'Thinking Station' will contain a permanent explanation of what it is and how it is supposed to work. It will also have several resources that change periodically. Each of the resources will promote thinking in some way.

Some content for the 'Thinking Station' may include:

Title:	The 'Thinking Station'
Statements:	The way to better thinking is to Think!
	Good Thinking needs Thinking About!
	Thinking does not wear out the brain!
	This is not the place to be given answers!
Explanation:	Please engage with this thinking station. It is intended to help you. It is not here to provide answers to questions but it is here to help you to develop your own thinking ability in your own way. Thinking more and thinking better will help you, not just at work, but in your personal life too.
	Please remember however, it is only you that can develop your own thinking and if this thinking station works it is because you have achieved something through your own efforts not because this thinking station has done anything.
	The thinking station should change each week for a period of time. However, please visit it more frequently than once a week if you like. The important things to take away from this station are not pieces of paper or things, but the thoughts that develop in your head.
Thought Explanation:	
	Please have a thought!
	Use a card to express any useful thoughts you may have. This is not a feedback or an ideas box but you may use it as such if you want to. Please have the conviction to take responsibility for your thought by making sure that you fill in the name box. Anonymous

contributions are not welcome and will not be used. You may however, choose to tick the no publicity box, in which case your thoughts will not be attributed to you if they are used.

Thoughts may be used to achieve the thing that they are intended to achieve or simply thought about.

Feedback Text:

Please take some time to provide feedback for this project. Without your feedback it will be difficult to make progress. This is an important part of the thinking station trial.

The area that is the home to the 'Thinking Station' is the place to put leaflets which explain brainstorming, lateral thinking etc. It is also the place to put a weekly puzzle and to ask others to suggest a puzzle for the next week etc. It may, from time to time, contain small gifts such as small puzzles etc, that staff can take home.

In fact, the thinking station can be the place for any resource which is intended to help develop the ability of people to think and to attend to problems and of course, to notice problems or potential improvements in the first place. It can be a visible component of the Innovation Scheme. Developing the thinking station will be an interesting challenge in itself.

4.9   A Cultural Example

On several occasions whilst studying knowledge in larger companies, I have come across the comment that the people there know how to do things but can't actually make them happen. It usually turned out that this was indeed true, they did know how to do things and the things in general, never happened. It seemed however, they actually only knew the mechanisms and did not know in a more general sense, how to make things happen. In some cases, this seemed to be because the people involved were perhaps technically focussed and missed other important project related elements such as the process of change.

On one occasion, some of the people involved with this difficulty were asked about what they thought could be causing the problem. Still other potential causes seemed obvious to an outsider. The list of potential contributors to the problem ended up as follows:

Information Overload	There is too much information for everything that needs to be done Can't find the bits really needed The work is too complicated to follow
Motivation	We can't be bothered. You don't get credit for avoiding problems - only solving them **Buy In** I don't agree with this
Resources	I am too busy other things interfere The job needs investment
Organisation	Poorly allocated work schedule No one is responsible for seeing that this is done People responsible have no authority I didn't know I was supposed to do this
Management	People don't do what they are supposed to do, what they are told to do I forgot about it
Leadership	When we decide what to do, that's when people start to debate it
Consequences	There are adverse consequences in doing this There will be staff reductions There will be budget cuts

Many of the causes listed above are closely related and some problems that in themselves can prevent progress, also lead to other problems that can also prevent progress, compounding the problem. For instance, a lack of resources may cause managers to ask people to do too much but not have the time to check that things are being done. The people doing too much may not have time or may forget and in general their motivation may suffer. They may then decide that they either don't agree with the task or don't agree that they should be doing it etc.

In other words, to make things happen, all of the potential problems stated above (and possibly some others) need to be addressed.

If one attempted to classify this whole set of problems that lead to the inability to make things happen one may conclude that the problem is business culture. For instance, why do people with a technical focus fail to acknowledge when they need help from first class managers and why do managers fail to see that simply giving an already heavily loaded person more work does not mean that any problem has been solved?

Referring to some of the cultural elements, attitudes and values discussed in section 4.1 reveals that most if not all of the problems stated above have simple cultural causes. For instance, the three potential problems with motivation can each be related to the cultural elements discussed in section 4.1, particularly elements c and d. The problems concerning making things happen can also be seen to require management to adopt the same cultural attitudes and values they would wish their staff to adopt.

The point about this actual example is that it can easily apply to the introduction of a programme for innovation. It is one thing to know and understand how to design and develop such a program but it is another thing to actually make it happen and then sustain it.

5. Assessing Innovation

The earlier research discussed in chapter 2 lead to the development of an innovation assessment tool. This was based on the requirements for innovation that were elicited from senior managers during the interview phases of two projects. The intention was to produce something which would be easy to use and would convey information as it was being used and as a result of analysis. The format chosen was a question and answer format where senior people within an organisation to be assessed, would answer questions about innovation related activities within the organisation. It was intended that the questions would actually cause the managers to consider their approach to innovation and even if no assessment was done, there would be considerable value in addressing the questions.

In the final Innovation Analyser tool, some supportive comment was provided along with each question. In many cases, this support was in the form of a video clip recorded by one of the senior managers participating in the project. At the end of the question answering session, some attempt was made to analyse the scores provided and produce a measure of performance in innovation for that organisation. Some options to improve were also suggested by the tool.

Initially, it will be useful to consider what this tool actually did and how it carried out analysis and produced recommendation. It will then be interesting to consider this assessment method with respect to other methods and then with respect to the innovation programme discussed earlier.

5.1 The P42 Innovation Analyser

A set of questions was derived from interview notes and comment. The questions were designed to uncover current working practice and to address the broad areas of Generate, Evaluate, Activate and Review. Management of Innovation was also investigated through the set of questions. Each of the broad areas was identified by their initial letter for convenience.

Generate   -   Generation of Ideas
Evaluate   -   Evaluation and Assessment of Ideas
Activate   -   Making Ideas work to improve the organisation
Review   -   Reviewing performance
Management   -   The performance of the Managers of Innovation

There were 32 questions in all and each could be considered within the G E A R M context. The questions themselves will now be listed along with an explanation and some help as to how scores should be assigned when the questions are answered. All scores are integers in the range 0 to 9.

5.1.1 Questions to Assess Innovation

Q1 Does the organisation have a clear definition for innovation?

It is important that the organisation knows what innovation is. There should be a definition available and senior managers at least, should be well aware of it. The actual content of the definition is not so important but it should cover the whole process from the creative generation of ideas to the successful implementation of a product, system or service.

Scoring: 0 for no definition at all and 9 for a well published and well known definition

Q2 Is innovation seen as a long or short term activity?

Innovation is a long term commitment for organisations. Short term reactive responses can have a limited effect in certain areas but are unlikely to support some of the key elements of innovation such as culture and environment.

Scoring: 0 for very short term, 9 for a permanent policy

Q3   Is there an organisation scheme to support innovation?
Some companies have a clear and explicit scheme that supports innovation. This will be something that has documentary support and that staff are fully aware of.
Scoring: 0 for no explicit scheme, 9 for fully verifiable and known scheme

Q4   Are senior managers promoters of innovation?
There are two issues to this question. Senior managers should visibly and explicitly promote organisational innovation through appropriate systems and practices. They should also implicitly promote innovation by encouragement, positive reinforcement and general staff support.
Scoring: 0 if there is no explicit of implicit support, 9 if both are evident.

Q5   How does the organisation manage innovation?
Managers should discuss innovation at their meetings. Innovation may be seen as an item on various management meeting agendas. Is the attitude of managers to innovation both positive and consistent?
Scoring: 0 if there is no innovation management, 9 if a clear strategy exists

Q6   Do certain staff have responsibility towards the process of innovation?
When an organisation is truly committed to a process, it is usually possible to be able to identify a person or group who are responsible for the development and general well being of the process. If it is not possible to find someone who is charged with the development of innovation, then a real organisational commitment must be suspect.
Scoring: 0 for no person or group responsibility, 9 explicit documented responsibility

Q7   To what degree does a culture of blame exist within the organisation?
Are staff hounded for their mistakes or is there a supportive, understanding atmosphere. There should be a desire to learn from mistakes and develop rather than to identify the culprit and persecute. This does not mean that mistakes should be encouraged or the person responsible not identified.
Scoring: 0 for an evident culture of blame, 9 for a fully supportive culture

Q8   Can staff act on their own initiative?
In many organisations, staff are discouraged from acting on their own initiative. Organisation procedures must be followed at all times even when staff can see mistakes. There must be a balance between a rigid authoritarian environment and a free for all. This balance, if correct, can encourage staff to develop and pioneer new and better systems for the organisation.
Scoring: 0 for a completely inflexible environment, 9 for the correct balance

Q9   What happens if an act of initiative goes wrong?
What is the organisations actual response when things go wrong? Is there evidence of an inquest to ensure lessons are learned or is there a 'witch hunt'? An analysis of what actually happens can be more revealing than a statement of policy.
Scoring: 0 for witch hunt, 9 for supportive analysis

Q10   What is the attitude of staff towards innovation?
When talking to individual staff members, is there evidence of new ideas and of alertness to improvement. Do staff want to make suggestions. It is clearly beneficial if staff see innovation as a way of moving the organisation forward rather than seeing it as only worthwhile if it directly benefits them.
Scoring: 0 for a negative or indifferent attitude, 9 for a positive encouraging attitude

Q11   Is there a clear and supportive staff development scheme in the organisation?
A well organised staff development scheme will be properly documented and staff will be aware of it. Staff will know how they can take advantage of the scheme. There will be a staff development officer in larger organisations or a person with staff development responsibilities in smaller organisations. There will be evidence of recent and older successful staff development activities.
Scoring: 0 for no policy, 9 for a fully developed successful policy

Q12 What proportion of staff are involved in some form of staff development?
If staff development is real and not simply a façade, there should be a reasonable proportion of staff engaged in some form or development activity. This could include studying on organised courses, attending short training programmes, attending conferences and seminars, using personal distance learning packages at work or work on a personal development project.
Scoring: 0 for no staff involved, 9 if 50% or more of staff are involved

Q13 Is staff development constrained to organisation directed study?
Staff development can be more effective if it is more open and free. Sometimes, organisations only want staff to develop in areas of direct relevance to their organisation or even to their job. This may mean that new opportunities go unexplored. A more open staff development attitude will pay longer term dividends.
Scoring: 0 for no development or strictly directed, 9 for a completely open policy

Q14 Do senior managers take advantage of staff development?
It is important that senior managers and even directors are still learning during their working lives. The type of study they engage in may be varied and may not be formal. However, some form or career development and knowledge development is desirable.
Scoring: 0 for no senior management study, 9 for clear evidence of development

Q15 How does the organisation view life long learning?
The organisation should have heard of the term 'life long learning' and should understand the implications of it. It should be possible to discuss this concept with senior managers and understand the organisation's positive response to it.
Scoring: 0 for no policy, 9 for a positive attitude and supporting evidence

Q16 Does the organisation believe that education supports innovation?
There is a strong general belief that education can support innovation. This is the reason why staff development and life long learning programmes have developed. If the organisation does not believe in education, its responses to the other concepts may mean little.
Scoring: 0 - education is considered unimportant, 9 - a positive attitude to education

Q17 Is there a constant flow of new ideas and suggestions from staff?
It should be possible to view records of suggestions made by staff over a long period. It should be possible to talk to staff that have made suggestions and elicit their feelings on the value of the process.
Scoring: 0 if no records can be found, 9 for detailed records and positive attitude

Q18 Is there a clear mechanism for the presentation of new ideas?
It should be possible to discover the process for ideas and suggestions and inspect the physical mechanisms that enable them.
Scoring: 0 for no scheme, 9 for a well publicised and effective scheme

Q19 How are new ideas received by senior staff?
Senior staff can have a positive or negative effect on the process of generating ideas by their attitude to them. If they brush them off or act indifferent, the instigator can be discouraged from the whole process. Likewise, if all ideas are ignored they will eventually not be produced. However, if staff are encouraged and thanked and the best ideas are acted upon, this will stimulate the process.
Scoring: 0 for a negative, off hand attitude, 9 for an encouraging active environment

Q20 Who gets the credit for a good idea?
In some cases, the supervisor or manager will aim to take some or all credit for ideas passed on by staff. This can be very annoying for the staff members. Senior staff should take credit for their own ideas and possibly for the amount of ideas generated by his/her section. The credit for each new idea should go to the originator. Interviews with staff and managers may be necessary to verify this.
Scoring: 0 for evidence of idea hijacking, 9 if all originators get the credit

Q21 What are the creators rewards for innovative ideas?
It is not always necessary to provide monetary reward for successful ideas. It is important however, that the originator feels that some justice has been done and the process is fair. If an idea is acclaimed to have saved (or made) the organisation a significant amount of money and the originator gets a pat on the back and then forgotten, this may be felt unfair. The reward, whether monetary or not, will influence future ideas.
Scoring: 0 for no reward or unfair system, 9 for a fair reward scheme

Q22 How are ideas evaluated?
Not all ideas will be useful or practical. It is necessary to have each idea considered by appropriate people using a set of assessment criteria. It may be possible to quickly select the ideas with the most potential and then use a more rigorous approach to identify the best ideas.
Scoring: 0 for no evaluation mechanism, 9 for a comprehensive scheme

Q23 Is the organisation open to new ideas from outside of the organisation?
Many organisations, particularly smaller ones, feel that they do not have time to search for new opportunities. However, there are many sources of opportunity for organisations including journals, the internet, trade organisations, business support groups, seminars, conferences, networking events etc. An organisation wishing to maintain a high level of innovation should make use of these sources.
Score: 0 for no activity in this area, 9 for an appropriate level of activity

Q24 How are ideas from outside the organisation imported and evaluated?
Assuming that ideas from outside the organisation find their way inside, there should be a regular process of consideration and assessment of these ideas. This process should be carried out regularly and formally and may be part of an initial filtering of the best or most appropriate ideas.
Scoring: 0 for no evaluation or no ideas from outside, 9 for a formal process

Q25 Is there a person or persons responsible for bringing in new ideas?
It is usually necessary to make someone responsible for any process. In this case, the person responsible could liaise with support organisations and ensure subscription to appropriate bodies and publications. He/she could ensure that appropriate organisation staff are informed about appropriate developments, activities and events. The person responsible would compile a regular report for consideration by senior evaluators.
Scoring: 0 for no responsible person, 9 for clearly identifiable responsibility

Q26 What happens to the best ideas?
When a good idea is identified it should be acted upon. The best way to verify this is to look for evidence of previous response to good ideas. It may be that an idea was investigated further but proved to be inappropriate. Or it could be that it was simply forgotten.
Scoring: 0 for no further action, 9 for rigorous assessment and further action

Q27 Can staff develop their own ideas, will they be given time and resources?
Staff who have good ideas may prove to be the best people to develop them. In some organisations, staff may be asked to do this but be given no extra resources. This can be demoralising. If an idea is worth developing, it is also worth investing in. If members of staff who have ideas simply end up with more work, this will eventually suppress the generation of ideas.
Scoring: 0 for no extra resources, 9 for properly resourced idea development

Q28 Is there an organisation scheme to pilot the best innovative ideas?
When a potentially successful idea is identified, it may be necessary to run a pilot project to properly evaluate it. This pilot project should contain all of the necessary elements for a comprehensive evaluation yet it should not commit the organisation to excessive expenditure. There will be a mechanism for carrying out pilot projects in organisations that regularly perform this task.
Scoring: 0 for no or ad hoc mechanism, 9 for fully documented procedure

Q29 Can the organisation correctly evaluate and validate pilot projects?
Has the organisation got a good record for the successful evaluation of pilot projects? This evaluation may lead to acceptance or rejection, but in either case, the decision will be based on logical and verifiable processes.
Scoring: 0 for no record, 9 for records of successful evaluation

Q30 Can the organisation generate backing to develop successful pilot schemes?
Does the organisation have a way of attracting investment capital for the development of sound projects resulting from innovative ideas? The organisation may be able to finance some projects itself.
Scoring: 0 for no backing available, 9 for a way of backing all good ideas

Q31 How is success fed back to the staff?
Success from innovation should be fed back to staff through high profile activities. These may include product launch events, publications, direct mailing to the homes of staff, meetings etc.
Score: 0 for no feedback, 9 for high profile feedback on all occasions.

Q32 Can examples of innovation becoming products or processes be found?
It should be possible to identify examples of past successful innovation within an innovative organisation. It may be argued that the innovation process has just started and no prior examples exist. If this is the case, then it could be the case that the process of innovation may be short term.
Scoring: 0 for no records, 9 for fully verified records of successful innovation

5.1.2 Placing the questions in context
The previous questions were the original 32 questions used in the Innovation Analyser. The following table separates the questions into categories and assigns priorities to each question where 1 is highest priority and 3 is the lowest.

Nº	Question	Priority	G E A R M
	Issues concerning definition:		
1	Does the organisation have a clear definition for innovation?	3	R
2	Is innovation seen as a long or short term activity?	3	R,M
	Management Related Issues:		
3	Is there an organisation scheme to support innovation?	2	A,M
4	Are senior managers promoters of innovation?	2	A,M
5	How does the organisation manage innovation?	3	A,M
6	Do certain staff have some responsibility towards the process of innovation?	2	A,M
	Issues related to organisation culture and environment:		
7	To what degree does a culture of blame exist within the organisation?	1	M
8	Can staff act on their own initiative?	2	M
9	What happens if an act of initiative goes wrong?	1	M
10	What is the attitude of staff towards innovation?	2	M
	Issues related to staff development:		
11	Is there a clear and supportive staff development scheme in the organisation?	2	M
12	What proportion of staff are involved in some form of staff development?	2	M
13	Is staff development constrained to organisation directed study?	3	M
14	Do senior managers take advantage of staff development?	3	M
15	How does the organisation view life long learning?	3	M
16	Does the organisation believe that education supports innovation?	3	M
	Issues related to the creation of Ideas:		
17	Is there a constant flow of new ideas and suggestions from staff?	2	G

18	Is there a clear mechanism for the presentation of new ideas?	1	E,M
19	How are new ideas received by senior staff?	2	E,M
20	Who gets the credit for a good idea?	1	G,M
21	What are the creator's rewards for innovative ideas?	3	G
22	How are ideas evaluated?	2	E
	Issues concerning an Open Door policy:		
23	Is the organisation open to new ideas from outside?	2	G
24	How are ideas from outside the organisation imported and evaluated?	3	E
25	Is there a person or persons responsible for bringing in new ideas?	1	G,M
	Issues related to the processing of Ideas:		
26	What happens to the best ideas?	2	A
27	Can staff develop their own ideas, will they be given time and resources?	2	G,M
28	Is there an organisation scheme to pilot the best innovative ideas?	2	A,M
	Issues related to projects and evaluation		
29	Can the organisation correctly evaluate and validate pilot projects?	2	R,M
30	Can the organisation generate backing to develop successful pilot schemes?	2	A
31	How is success fed back to the staff?	3	R,M
	Issues related to implementation:		
32	Can examples of innovation becoming products or processes be found?	3	A

The right hand column of the table shows which element of innovation, G E A R M, the question is relevant to. Some of the questions are thought relevant to more than one of the innovation areas.

5.1.3 *Computing a Score*
The score allocated to G E A R M, was calculated based on an average score for the questions involved. In a few cases, some of the questions were thought to be more relevant to the issue than the others and the weighting of these questions have been increased as part of the average calculation. Values were computed as follows.

$G = ((Q17*2) + Q20 + Q21 + Q23 + (Q25*2) + Q27) / 8$

$E = (Q18 + Q19 + (Q22*2) + Q24) / 5$

$A = (Q3 + Q4 + Q5 + Q6 + Q26 + (Q28*2) + (Q30*2) + (Q32*2)) / 11$

$R = (Q1 + Q2 + (Q29*2) + Q31) / 5$

$M = (Q2*2)+Q3+(Q4*2)+Q5+(Q6*2)+(Q7*2)+Q8+Q9+(Q10*2)+Q11+Q12+Q13+Q14+Q15+$
$Q16+(Q18*2)+(Q19*2)+Q20+(Q25*2)+Q27+(Q28*2)+(Q29*2)+Q31$

33

In addition to the separate scores for each area of innovation, it is possible to calculate and assess an overall score.

Scores can be awarded to each of the 32 checklist items. They will be in the range from 0 to 9, with 9 being the best score and 0 being no score for that item. With this simple computation, the highest score reflect the most innovative organisations. However, qualifiers were included for a more in depth analysis.

Simple additive scores can range from 0 → 288 (32 x 9)

Realistic answers to questions are unlikely to lead to scores in excess of 230.

A score of 230 represents an innovative organisation that can still improve. A score of 288 represents an organisation that is not facing up to reality.

Scores are more likely to be much less than 230.

An organisation answering the questions, with a reasonable degree of honesty, which has a lot of scope for improvement, may expect to score around 60.

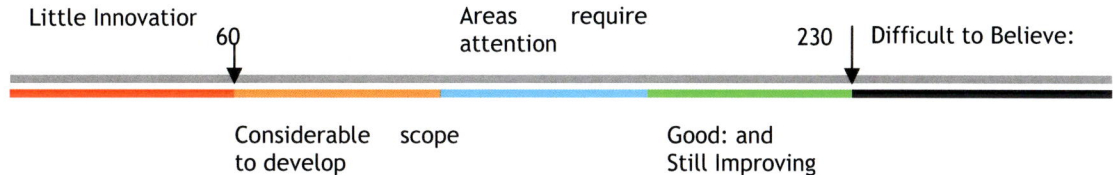

Little Innovatior   Areas   require   230   Difficult to Believe:
60   attention

Considerable   scope   Good: and
to develop   Still Improving

5.1.4 Providing Feedback

The value of using the innovation analyser was planned to be from facing the questions that were being asked and for each question, considering how a particular organisation responded. However, although this position is probably justifiable, some actual feedback in the form or conclusion was required. The feedback provided was based on the scores and the values for G E A R M, computed using the formulae given in section 5.1.3.

The following text was provided as feedback concerning performance in each of the G E A R M areas. The score would be in the range of 0 to 9 and the value 'V' reflects this score for each of the text options shown.

Generate

$V < 4$	Idea generation is not well controlled. It is possible to design schemes that can cause improvement. These may include reward, involvement and general encouragement.
$V >= 4$ & < 6	The generation of ideas needs to be developed further. Staff involvement and encouragement and a well designed mechanism are key elements.
$V >= 6$	Idea generation seems established. It is important to monitor progress and look for improvement.

Evaluate

$V < 4$	Evaluation of ideas is important both to encourage staff and to recognise ideas of high potential. An experienced group or panel can meet periodically to evaluate new ideas and suggestions.
$V >= 4$ & < 6	Evaluation should be a more formal process and properly managed. Selecting inappropriate ideas or rejecting good ideas can both be costly mistakes.
$V >= 6$	It is important to maintain the process of evaluation and retain the experience of evaluators.

Activate

$V < 4$	If ideas are wasted this will stifle the whole innovation process. Although it is not easy to turn ideas into products or processes it is important to have a sound policy and mechanism in place. Help is available from many sources.
$V >= 4$ & < 6	It is necessary to develop and formalise the process of taking an idea forward to a successful product or service. Standard methods and examples of good practice are available.
$V >= 6$	Turning ideas into products or services is not easy. A good track record provides confidence for the whole innovation process and valuable experience.

Review

$V < 4$	Unless lessons are learned from success and (more importantly) from failure, an organisation can waste time and money. All stages of the innovation process must be reviewed.
$V >= 4$ & < 6	Every project should have a formal review phase where lessons are learned and improvements are suggested. Review should be well managed and its outputs acted upon.
$V >= 6$	It should be possible to clearly show why a project was considered successful. It should also be possible to explain precisely why a project fails. Learning from mistakes and recording good practice create continuous improvement.

Manage

V < 4 The management of the innovation process really requires strengthening. This includes having a documented innovation scheme and a clear policy on staff development.

V >= 4 & < 6 Developing a more effective and robust approach to innovation management and to staff development could pay dividends. This may include producing separate but linked management strategies for the components of innovation.

V >= 6 Managing the process of innovation is as important as managing the business. It is important to evaluate the management of the process as well as the process itself.

Text was also provided in order to create a simple action plan. Text was generated in the same way as previously shown where comment for each of the areas G E A R M was provided based on the score 'V' for that area.

Generate

V < 4 Devise a staff suggestion scheme and attach it to a reward or acknowledgement framework.

V >= 4 & < 6 An improved staff suggestion scheme is required with section managers responsible for the performance of staff within their area.

V >= 6 No Action: Don't Print

Evaluate

V < 4 Form a team that meets regularly to consider suggestions and rank them. Have back up groups of specialists who can be called on to evaluate the more technical or specific suggestions.

V >= 4 & < 6 Make sure that an evaluation team that considers suggestions is actually doing its job. Place this scheme within a suitable management framework.

V >= 6 No Action: Don't Print

Activate

V < 4 Keep thorough records of potentially strong suggestions and make sure suggestions are allocated to a suitable department for implementation.

V >= 4 & < 6 Make sure that management processes perform regular checks on suggestions that have been approved to ensure their implementation.

V >= 6 No Action: Don't Print

Review

V < 4 The team that evaluates suggestions could also review implementation of successful ones. This will ensure that expertise for innovation is built up within this group.

V >= 4 & < 6 The output from the review process must have an outlet. A senior manager should be responsible for the overall innovation scheme and ensure that such outputs are acted upon.

V >= 6 No Action: Don't Print

Manage

V < 4 Devise a written company innovation policy along with definition. Make a senior manager directly responsible for the success of this policy and check on progress at least once per quarter initially.

V >= 4 & < 6 Identify a formal innovation management structure which includes a senior manager responsible, suggestion schemes, evaluation and review team performance and overall improvement. Invest in this scheme if required.

V >= 6 No Action: Don't Print

The general idea was that the assessment of performance would be provided as a direct result of interacting with the questions. The simple action plan was intended to be printed and taken away for review.

5.2 Analysing the Analyser

A software version of the P42 Innovation Analyser described in section 5.1 was developed for use in industry. It was used extensively by a firm of business consultants in Lancashire and by at least one regional Business Link group. All returned positive feedback concerning the analyser. It was primarily used by consultants working with business owners and managers as a way to get the innovation process started. The consultants using the software said that the business managers received it very well. It is reasonable to conclude that the P42 Innovation Analyser was well received by those who used it and by those that it was used to help. But what was its value?

1. Probably the main value of the P42 Innovation Analyser was:
2. It identified separate elements about innovation
3. It allowed business managers to think about specific instances of the business performance
4. It allowed business to see where progress and improvement could be made
5. It gave consultants an objective way to conduct innovation consultancy
6. It provided a step by step approach to innovation assessment
7. It provided conclusion and advice that could be challenged and contextualised

These are not insignificant claims for the analyser but they do not really address any procedure or process for innovation. It is interesting that the analyser offers no real process for managers to implement, just as set of individual elements that could be translated into actions based on honest answers to the questions about each element. The analyser probably offered 32 opportunities for a business to improve, because there were 32 questions.

When analysis of the answers was undertaken, the questions were seen as contributions to five component parts of innovation, generate, evaluate, activate, review and manage. This could be seen as a process but was not introduced as such. Managers, with the help of the consultant, could see in which of 32 areas they were deficient, in which of 5 basic innovation functions they were deficient and how they scored overall.

The claim is made that whilst these things do not really make an objective business approach to innovation, they do provide an excellent place at which to start moving any organisation towards becoming an innovative organisation. Making progress after that will require the more detailed understanding of innovation that is offered in this work.

At the moment, I have offered a brief analysis of the analyser, It would be interesting to compare this analyser with at least one other before drawing any firm conclusions.

5.2.1 The DTI Innovation Analyser.

The Department of Trade and Industry in the United Kingdom provides an innovation analyser or assessor (Checked on September 2008) at the web location:
http://www.innovation.gov.uk/self_assessment/home.asp?p=assessment
This analyser seems to be intended to perform the same function as the P42 innovation analyser. It is internet based and has 32 questions. Many of the questions are similar in nature to the ones in the P42 analyser but they probably relate more to employee behaviour and customer interaction than the P42 ones. The DTI analyser asks users to agree or disagree with statements made rather than to provide a number representing an answer to a question. The results that the user provides for the DTI analyser are:
Strongly Disagree   --   Disagree   --   Agree   --   Strongly Agree

The DTI analyser provides an overall score and statement to go with it and also provides analysis in three categories. These categories are:

Inspire   --   Create   --   Connect

Each of the three categories is sub divided into three areas where a percentage score is offered. The separate categories are:

Inspire
Building a culture of innovation   =   score%

Stretching to achieve	=	score%
Our people make us what we are	=	score%
Create		
Teaming with networks	=	score%
Hands ready top management	=	score%
Making it happen	=	score%
Connect		
Connecting with the customer	=	score%
New market vision	=	score%
Knowing how to win	=	score%

If 'strongly agree' is offered to all statements, the overall score is 100% and you are informed that you are a level 4 organisation. The overall score separates users into levels 1, 2, 3 and 4, where level 4 is the most innovative organisation. If you offer 'strongly disagree' to all questions then you are a level 1 organisation scoring 0% in all three categories. Clearly these extremes will never be arrived at with honest answers, they are only offered here to show the range of analysis provided by the tool.

Clearly the formulae that provide the analytical values are not available but this is not really important for this consideration. Contrasting the DTI Analyser with the, probably older, P42 analyser can be seen most effectively by considering the output categories.

Inspire   --   Create   --   Connect

Generate --   Evaluate --   Activate   --   Review   --   Manage

I would suggest that it is easier for an organisation to relate to the P42 categories than to the DTI categories, at least from an Innovation Management perspective. However, this observation is not an attempt to find that one tool is better than another. Both tools fulfil the need that they were intended for. Considering the benefits claimed for the P42 analyser and repeated here:

1. It identified separate elements about innovation
2. It allowed business managers to think about specific instances of the business performance
3. It allowed business to see where progress and improvement could be made
4. It gave consultants an objective way to conduct innovation consultancy
5. It provided a step by step approach to innovation assessment
6. It provided conclusion and advice that could be challenged and contextualised

Both tools satisfy these perceived benefits although I would argue that one satisfies item 1 better than the other. This is personal judgement however and I will leave the reader to agree or disagree and to consider which does it best if this is felt to be necessary.

5.2.2 The value of Analysers
Considering the DTI analyser has reinforced the opinion, my opinion, that analysers of this sort do provide some real benefit to organisations that intend to develop innovation on a permanent basis but are not sure how to get going. Analysers show what things can be done straight away and the analysis provides some justification for doing them. Since I was not involved with the creation of the DTI tool, it is difficult for me to comment objectively on its component parts. However, it does seem to fulfil many of the claims that are made about the P42 analyser but possibly in a slightly different way. One important point to note is that the DTI tool is still up and running now (or at least it was when this was written).

The P42 analyser was designed with the involvement of a number of senior managers in a broad range of organisation. This meant that, even though it did not promote a process for innovation, the questions that it used to assess innovation were categorised in a process oriented way. This in turn means that the analysis started from the generation of ideas, through the evaluation of ideas and on to the activation or implementation of those ideas. It included a review and a management phase to imply that innovation would require some control, at least at the organisational level. This meant that the P42 analyser offered exactly what it was intended to offer, immediate help, but also, by implication at least, offered some framework for building the future of innovation within the organisation.

It is worth pointing out that the original software version of the P42 analyser contained a large number of video clips recorded by three of the managers from three companies. These clips provided clarification for each question but were in fact, simply comment extracted from recorder interviews with those people. This addition was included, at least in part, because feedback from early workshops showed that people in business liked to hear, first hand (well at least by video clip), what other successful managers were doing and what they thought.

The P42 Innovation Analyser offered real value to organisations wishing to take the first steps down the path to becoming truly innovative organisations. Once an organisation has formed its own policy for innovation and put this policy into practice, there may be little need for an analyser like the P42 Analyser. However, there will still be a need for assessment of innovation as part of the process of improving it. After having said that, the group responsible for innovation in a large organisation may still prefer to use a tool like the P42 analyser to 'break the ice' when rolling out the innovation policy to new parts of the business. In this case, the group may prefer to design their own analyser and hopefully the information contained in section 5.1 will be useful in this.

5.3   Improving Analysis
The analysers discussed previously are based on the reflective answers to questions or thoughts of managers of organisations. This sort of analysis is valuable even though it relies on probably biased opinion. People answering the questions know or soon find out, that if they are not honest with their answers, then the subsequent analysis is of no value to them. As discussed previously, the analysis provides some guidance as to what to think about when developing an innovation programme. However, once innovation is underway, there is probably a need for analysis which is more objective than that discussed previously. This means, analysis based on some objective measures where data can justify the values assigned to questions etc. This in turn means that we must consider what sort of things should be measured for a more mature innovation scheme.

A large proportion of the diagram for Continuous Improvement developed in section 3.2.1 was devoted to the measurement of the process that was to be the target of innovative improvement. This element of an innovation process was again discussed in section 3.6. Therefore, at least one set of things that a more mature innovation policy should measure are the business process, products and services that are to be the target for innovation.

The business process, in its general sense, covering products and services, exists to sustain and improve a successful organisation. In many organisations, success means profit and market share etc. Ultimately an innovation scheme should have an impact on the success of the organisation.

If the innovation scheme itself is to be sustained, managers must know whether it is working or not and if it is working, how well it's working. The performance of the innovation process is linked to, or should be linked to the business process and business success. However in order to for instance, improve innovation, there needs to be some guidance as to what elements of it can or should be changed. If changes are made then there needs to be some feedback to determine if the change is having the desired effect. Ultimately this effect may be seen in the business process, products and services but there needs to be some way of linking this effect to the working of innovation.

5.3.1 Measuring the Business Process
In section 4.4 it was stated that the best thing to do, if possible, would be to measure everything. However, it was acknowledged that this is likely to place a considerable administrative burden on an organisation, so much of a burden that it would probably never be done. Some more achievable measurement targets were identified in section 4.4, these were:
 ➢   production rates (of components and systems)   - Increase
 ➢   stoppage delays   - Reduce

➢ breakages	- Reduce
➢ bottlenecks	- Increase
➢ profit	- Increase

Clearly, targets for measurement will not only depend on the sort of activity which is being undertaken by the organisation, they will also depend on the objectives of any specific business process. For instance, a production shop is unlikely to have any involvement with a sales department so measuring sales is not likely to be a factor in the performance of the production shop. However, the production targets for the production shop are likely to be key factors.

It will be necessary to set targets for measurement for specific organisational functions rather than set generic targets for any organisation. However, it is possible to provide some guidance as to how to select targets.

The first thing that should be made clear is the extent of the activity to which the innovation scheme is being applied. If this is the whole organisation then it may be important to consider whether divisions of that organisation need to be looked at separately. Even if this is done, some linkage between departments should be catered for.

The next thing is to consider what the organisation, or section of it, is supposed to achieve. This should be more than, make a profit. It should include the thing that is being done in order to generate income. In a manufacturing environment, the main income generator is likely to be the things being manufactured and it is likely that to be able to manufacture these things more efficiently will increase profit. In a business service environment it is also likely that the main aim is to make a profit but this will be done by selling successful business services to others. Therefore, the success of the business service and the efficiency with which it is delivered will affect the profit. If the organisation is a sales outlet, then the more efficiently it can sell, the more profit is likely to be generated.

Efficiency is therefore a key indicator of the business process. Efficiency is measured by considering the outputs of the process with respect to the inputs to the process. It therefore follows that some of the key things to be measured are those which will provide a comprehensive and thorough calculation of efficiency. A cautionary note here is that efficiency is a full term part of organisational success. Too many organisations make cuts to improve efficiency only to find that the longer term success of the business is threatened, a point raised in section 3.4. This really relates back to the innovation process itself and which ideas are seen to be ultimately beneficial, making the point that the consequences of ideas or the side effects of ideas should be given careful consideration. Using efficiency as an important measure of organisational success is not wrong, but some people apply it incorrectly or even naïvely.

When people are a significant part of a business process, it can be difficult to fully understand what affects efficiency. For instance, stormy weather could affect efficiency, having the workplace too hot in summer or too cold in winter may affect efficiency, shocking items in the news may affect efficiency, business announcements may affect efficiency and unfortunately, a whole range of things that may not be predictable in advance. So the idea developed in section 4.4 of measuring everything is probably just too difficult.

What may be possible however is to measure the core indicators of efficiency such as production rates, failure rates, staff sickness etc. and monitor these on practically a daily basis. When deviation from a norm is noticed then the records should show what the probable cause of the deviation was. Now it would be possible to include the shocking news item, a serious outbreak of flu or a serious failure of a machine etc. Now the records would not only show the business process in a way that improvements to it would be noticed, they would also show likely reasons for changes in the process outputs. Therefore it may become evident that installing a better air conditioning system would actually be cost effective for instance.

5.3.2 Measuring Success
If a serious innovation initiative is to take place in an organisation, it will probably be done in order to make the organisation more successful. Whilst any individual idea may have little effect on the overall success of an

organisation, the cumulative effect of many small innovative ideas may ultimately have a significant effect on success.

The data from the measurement of overall organisational success should therefore be available to those responsible for the innovation process, just as data concerning the monitoring of innovation itself should be available to the most strategic business managers and directors.

It is not within the context of this work to consider how to measure overall business success but a few comments are irresistible. I remember hearing a very successful business person in the North West of England saying over coffee in a business meeting, that although there were many important things to consider in business, profit is the only really important thing. Whilst many business leaders, particularly successful ones, would agree with that, I am afraid I cannot. At the beginning of the 21st Century, we are beginning to see what effect that attitude is going to have on our whole way of life as human beings and all other life on the planet. As we begin to witness this, we can watch documentaries which show how our early ancestors were able to live and work in harmony with nature, preserving it as they lived off it and never greedily taking more than they needed. Some business leaders will say that such concerns are not their responsibility; they contribute to the economic wealth of a society. But businesses are now amongst the most powerful organisations in the world and if they cannot take any responsibility for the world that we all live in, then who will?

This diversion was simply intended to attempt to show that profit may not be the only measure of success for organisations, or rather businesses, in the future. I suppose that all things could ultimately be translated into profit if all consumers redirected their purchasing power towards organisations that did most for the environment for instance, but at present at least, humans seem incapable of doing this on any large scale. Maybe it is up to those who are intelligent enough to make it to the top of large organisations, to take on more responsibility for the whole planet and human kind, and the future of life on the planet.

5.3.3 Measuring the Innovation Process

A large manufacturing company in the UK measured the number of ideas submitted to its idea scheme as a rough measure of the innovation process. It was known how many ideas were put forward by staff working in each manager's area. This meant that more senior managers were able to look at how staff in general were interacting with the scheme and how much facilitation of the scheme was being done by each area manager.

The innovation process diagram shown in section 3.6.1 indicates that the innovation process could be measured in a more detailed way than just the presentation of ideas. It suggests that it may be possible to measure the source of ideas with respect to the way ideas are developed. It suggests that ideas can be measured at the filter process so that it is known how many good, reasonable or naïve ideas are presented and which ideas are getting through the filter process. It may also be useful to measure the resources being used by the filter process. The diagram suggests that it will be possible and useful to measure the number of ideas being implemented and the scale of these ideas and how many of them require investment and what the return on investment is likely to be.

Each person or group submitting an idea should receive some feedback to explain what is happening with the idea. If the idea is a good one then there may be several points of feedback, the first one stating that the idea has been judged to have merit and will be considered further. If the idea is rejected at the beginning of the filter process then the feedback may explain why this has been done, certainly thank the person or group for the idea and maybe pass back any helpful comment concerning this and future ideas that the person or group may submit.

A valuable addition to this more detailed measuring approach would be to periodically (maybe annually) survey staff to find out what they think of the innovation process. For instance:

Do staff think that putting forward ideas is easy and they are encouraged to do so.
    This relates to the number of ideas being submitted and whether this can be improved.
Do staff feel that ideas they put forward are getting used

The opinion can be tested against the numbers or proportions actually getting used to discover whether opinion is in line with what is actually happening.

Do staff feel that they get useful feedback when they have submitted an idea

There will be records of the feedback provided to staff to compare against the impression that staff have concerning this feedback.

Do staff feel that the right people get credit for ideas

There should be records of who submitted ideas and who receives any acknowledgement.

Do staff feel that they are rewarded properly for good ideas.

The actual rewards or recognition can be compared with the impression of staff.

Are staff aware of the business improvements caused by good ideas from staff

This relates to the overall feedback to staff from the innovation scheme and may be at least one good measure of how sustainable the scheme is.

Do staff feel that the business improvements makes their position more secure

This will be another good indicator of sustainability.

A more intensive innovation monitoring scheme will use more organisational resources. Clearly managers would want to monitor the value coming from the innovation process itself against the resources that are required to maintain it. However, without at least some maintenance, the innovation process is likely to be unsustainable. But the investment in the sustainability of an innovation process must be weighed against the value that the process is providing for the business.

5.3.4 The Problems with Measurement

One of the biggest problems with measurement is in selecting the particular components to measure. As stated in section 4.4, there is the issue of selecting the right ones so that the scheme is properly evaluated and matures to deliver its intended goals. However, there is the issue of selecting components of a scheme to measure that are perhaps easy to measure and also fairly isolated. Once components are measured and it becomes a goal or a target to improve performance, there is a tendency to work out ways to improve the component being measured rather than improve the thing that measurement is being carried out for. For instance, if the number of ideas is the main or only measure and maybe there is some reward or recognition for managers whose area submits the most ideas, then there may be a tendency to submit any and all ideas no matter what their value is. This may actually create a bigger burden on the filter process without creating any more useful ideas. Similarly, if there is pressure on the filter process because it is seen to be rejecting a high proportion of ideas, then there may be pressure on the people working in that part of the process to accept more ideas and therefore to implement more ideas with questionable predicted benefit. This may have its own consequences but neither situation is good for innovation.

Without measurement, managers may have no way of knowing if the innovation scheme is working and no way of making it more effective in the future. However, the idea that it is possible to single out one element of a measuring scheme for improvement without considering what effect this will have on the rest of the scheme is naïve and possibly dangerous. Deciding how to improve innovation based on the measures used to assess it will be a complex task and should be given careful consideration by managers.

It would not be uncommon for a manager to select a broad measurement target that would cover the general area of innovation without being too specific. Such a target could be the submission of ideas since this element of innovation is a key element for the whole process. The manager may then decide to monitor the idea submission process more carefully than the measurement suggests. He or she may decide to hold periodic meetings with other senior staff to discuss idea submission and ask for views about how well it was going. In this way, the overall manager could feel that although the target for measurement is quite weak, the control that is exercised over this target makes the resulting innovation control scheme fit for purpose. This sort of management control of a process could be viewed as flexible and adaptable since it relies on one general measurement coupled with continuous monitoring by and feedback from responsible staff. The problem with it is that if the senior manager becomes distracted with other issues then the measurement process could revert back to the rather rough idea submission scheme that does not get properly monitored.

Even the broad target that is tightly controlled by managers is likely to imply greater complexity in the measurement scheme. For instance, it is easy to imagine that during a meeting of the type just discussed, someone is likely to ask how many ideas are being accepted, or what proportion of ideas submitted lead to some business benefit, or where are the best ideas coming from, or how long is it taking to evaluate ideas etc. All of this implies the existence of a more informal and detailed measurement process that takes place in parallel with the formal single measurement. Unfortunately, instead of using actual figures for the answer to, what proportion of ideas lead to business benefit, for instance, the answer may come from an opinion of one or more of the managers at the meeting.

Designing a measurement scheme for innovation which supports the innovation process and its development without adding undesirable side effects is a difficult task and one that must be done within the context of the business that it is to operate in.

5.4   Using Assessment to Sustain Innovation

The question of the sustainability of the innovation process emerged in section 5.3 when discussing measurement. The problem with many organisational projects is that when there is activity, funded by the project, there is usually progress. When the project completes and the intensive activity is removed from that area of the organisation, then progress is likely to begin to decline. This is also true of new initiatives, probably because with a new initiative, there is intensive activity at the beginning to promote it. New initiatives are often successful at the beginning and then begin to decline as people become more familiar with the initiative and as activity within it declines. This is the problem of sustainability, activity and familiarity.

The familiarity issue has been addressed in section 4.3 when looking at practical steps that can be taken in developing a business innovation scheme. The issue was considered during the discussion of the environment in section 4.7 and the 'Thinking Station' in section 4.8. Comments within these sections were intended to help prevent the innovation scheme from stagnating and becoming forgotten.

The activity issue was considered graphically in the new innovation process in section 3.6.1 and has been the main focus of discussion in section 5.3 concerning the continuous improvement of the innovation scheme. This showed that measurement or assessment can be a good way to ensure the sustainability of innovation and to ensure that the innovation process itself is the subject of continuous activity.

An on going scheme of measurement analysis and improvement of the innovation process and good quality feedback from it, can work in parallel with the innovation process itself to create a dynamic and improving scheme that is able to adapt to change and new business demands and provide a permanent service for the organisation. Sustainability should be built into the design of the original scheme and assessment will play no small part in this.

To ensure sustainability of the innovation process the issues of activity and familiarity must be addressed.

5.4.1 Addressing the Activity Issue

The activity issue simply means ensuring that there is some activity always taking place within the innovation process. A fully functioning innovation process is the key to addressing the activity issue. Having a fully functioning innovation process is likely to mean that certain staff have permanent responsibilities to deliver parts of the innovation process as a core part of their job. The definition of responsibility for individual staff is likely to depend very heavily on the size of the organisation that is implementing the scheme and the scale of resource which the organisation can allocate to innovation. However, whatever the scale involved, the assignment of permanent, monitored responsibility is a key factor in ensuring that regular activity takes place within the innovation scheme.

Another way of promoting activity on a more permanent basis is to incorporate an automated system within the process. An automated system may be a computer package that can automatically collect data from the innovation process, analyse the data, format results and deliver these to managers responsible for innovation. This would mean that managers get regular reports based on verifiable data which shows how the innovation process is functioning. Dips in performance or trends that show a gradual reduction of activity can then be addressed as soon as they are noticed.

In short, one element concerned with creating a sustainable innovation process is ensuring that something is always going on within the process.

5.4.1 Addressing the Familiarity Issue

Familiarity seems to be a natural phenomenon. Even the human nervous system operates in such a way that regular and on going stimulation of a particular sense is gradually ignored by the central nervous system. A hot bath feels less hot when one has been in it for a minute or two and someone walking into a building at normal temperature after being outside in the cold for some time may feel hot for a little while then begin to feel that the building temperature is correct.

When an exciting new project is started and people are asked to do new things that hopefully interest them, they are likely to put quite a lot of effort in and give rather more attention to the new project than the other things they were doing before that project was introduced. However, as the project becomes more familiar when it has been operating for some time, people will pay less attention to it, find it less interesting and put less effort into it than they did when it was new. This is simply something that humans do and that fact needs to be acknowledged.

Although we may acknowledge the fact, an organisation cannot simply accept that a newly introduced scheme will only work for a little while before it has to be scrapped. This would imply that all human activity would eventually fail and this is clearly not the case. It was shown in section 4.3 that there are things that can be done to reduce the effects of familiarity and therefore help to ensure that projects are more sustainable. Perhaps the largest factor associated with sustainability is probably motivation (section 2.5).

The odd thing about familiarity is that people seem to prefer familiarity and dislike change (in general), yet tend to pay less attention to things that are familiar than they might to new or novel things. This does not mean all people behave like this; it is simply suggesting that this is a general tendency. People are often concerned or frightened by unfamiliar things and by changes that remove the things they are familiar with and replace them with new or unknown things. It seems that whilst people in general may prefer the familiar to the unfamiliar, they also pay less attention to familiar things and maybe even neglect the familiar. Yet people can also be motivated to do a good job and they can be motivated to want to improve and they can be motivated towards success. Theories of motivation (section 2.5.1) attempt to explain why people may behave this way and what conditions may encourage such behaviour. Motivation has been sighted as a key factor for innovation throughout the earlier parts of this book. It seems that motivation is probably a key factor for sustainability. Sustainability that is, of innovation, but motivation is likely to be a key factor for the sustainability of any project.

For a particular organisation it could be useful to ask why staff carry out their duties successfully every day and what motivates them to do this. Is it that they do it because they are paid and they feel that it is fair to work for the pay they receive? It may be because they are concerned about the consequences of not working hard, such as criticism or even dismissal. Whatever the reason that people in a particular work place normally carry out their duties, this could also work for sustainability. For a project to become sustainable, it needs to be seen by staff as part of their duty. This may mean staff are taking on new duties when a new project or initiative is introduced. A potential problem here is that staff could feel they are constantly expected to take on new duties without ever relinquishing other duties. They may feel that they are being compelled to work harder and harder for no extra reward or their work load is becoming unmanageable because of the additional duties.

The implication here is that for a project or initiative to be sustainable, there needs to be time allocated for it within the working day. Maybe efficiency savings in one area could release resources to be applied to another new area or maybe the introduction of a new initiative means that something else has to go or that more staff need to be recruited etc.

If a new project or initiative is simply introduced and then left to run its course, it is likely to become unsustainable. Familiarity is likely to cause a gradual decline in interest in the project and therefore in purposeful activity on the project. If however, the new project or initiative is designed so that there are resources that are available for it, there is constant activity associated with it and staff begin to see it as part of the working day rather than as something new, then it is more likely to be a sustainable project or initiative.

6. Managing Innovation and Making it Work

This chapter will consider how the information in the previous chapters can be brought together to design a useful and sustainable innovation scheme which will provide real business benefit. But before dealing with the details of the programme, it is important to consider at least one point that was discussed in several of the earlier meetings and interviews. The point is, there needs to be someone in charge or someone responsible for the innovation programme. This person will ultimately drive the programme, sustain it and improve it. The person will be able to provide data that senior managers need to assess innovation and how well it is working and will be the one that will respond to criticism of the programme, for instance, excessive cost compared with modest delivery. Someone's personal standing or reputation will depend on the success or failure of the innovation programme.

The amount of time an organisation allocates to managing the innovation process will depend on the proportion of overall turnover that such a resource represents and the importance with which the organisation views innovation. Clearly, a very small company may not be able to employ a full time manager responsible for innovation alone whilst a very large organisation may decide to employ an innovation team or department headed by a fairly senior manager.

The responsibility of the innovation manager will be to implement, sustain and develop the innovation scheme and all associated activities. This will include monitoring the success of the scheme, accessing process measures, encouraging staff, perhaps through their line managers, to become actively involved with the scheme and maybe most importantly, to oversee the right environment, or culture for innovation within the organisation. The innovation managers will interface with many other parts of the organisation, both reporting to and requesting action from other managers. Success for the innovation team will mean success for line managers and success for the whole organisation. All will be seeking to achieve the same goals.

It is interesting to consider the implications of having an innovation manager. In most organisations, managers are responsible for ensuring that some part of a business or organisation is running correctly and delivering its targets. They each may play a larger or smaller part in ensuring that the organisation is achieving its goals. An innovation manager on the other hand, will be responsible for ensuring that the organisation gets better at what it does and/or develops new methods, new systems, new products etc. This latter responsibility may be assigned to others such as the board of directors but the innovation manager could expect his or her work to lead to innovative ideas which may form the basis of items that ultimately the board would wish to consider. The innovation manager's first responsibility however is to ensure that the organisation improves.

In certain situations, an organisation may need to adapt to external changes. These may come from the market, from legislation, from technological development or even from new opportunity. Innovation will play a part in such changes and the innovation manager's role in this could be significant. For instance, if the Chief Executive needs to discuss forthcoming legislative changes that will affect the company's main product, the innovation manager, with the assistance of records and line managers, may be able to put together the very best consultation team that the organisation can aspire to.

In summary, someone needs to be made responsible for and accountable for innovation within an organisation and be given the authority to implement and develop the innovation scheme. That person needs to be given the resources to carry out this role within the organisation.

6.1   What aspects of Innovation can be managed?

It is doubtful whether one can make people have innovative ideas, and when they do have them, it is doubtful they can be made to share those ideas. However, there is a lot about innovation in an organisation that can be managed and more than this, there is probably a lot that must be managed if innovation is to succeed as an organisational long term objective.

Any process can be managed and the innovation process is no exception. In section 4.5.1 consideration was given to the idea that if things were left alone, innovation would happen anyway and the idea that the whole thing needs a process or management may be misdirected. In that discussion, it was seen that innovation would not happen in any case if barriers existed to prevent it happening. More than this however, if an organisation is looking to improve through innovation then the innovation process needs to be given all of the help and support that can be given.

Although it may be true that people cannot be forced to have ideas or to submit them, they can be encouraged to do so and the way they do this can be facilitated. Once an idea has emerged then it can be carried forward through a process and this process can and should be managed. It is quite likely, in an organisation that does not have a managed process for innovation, that many good ideas will be lost because they will never be implemented. Clearly this may not be true in quite small organisations where senior managers are closely involved with daily production activities etc. But in general, a managed process for innovation will ensure that innovation works better.

The flow of the innovation process will be managed by the innovation manager. He or she may set targets within the process and may allocate the delivery of separate targets to other people. For instance, it was stated that one company set individual managers targets for the submission of ideas. This could be done here. Carefully chosen targets concerning other aspects of innovation may be needed. For instance, it was noted that if the target for filtering a higher proportion of successful ideas was set then this may cause inappropriate ideas to get through the filter process. However, targets related to how long an idea waits, relative to its complexity, before it is evaluated should be set so that ideas are not left waiting for approval. Also monitoring and improving the feedback provided to those submitting ideas should be carried out and the time between idea submission and receiving some initial feedback should be a minimum.

Targets are not the only way or maybe not even the best way to manage the innovation process. There is no substitute for having intelligent, knowledgeable, well motivated staff working within the innovation process to ensure it is successful and that it improves. The manager's job is to make sure this happens.

One of the interesting comments made above is that related to having knowledgeable staff working in the innovation process. What exactly should knowledgeable staff working within the innovation process actually know? Again it is up to the managers of the area to make sure this is known and that staff have the opportunity to acquire the necessary knowledge. Personally, I would recommend a knowledge study here using the Knowledge Structure Mapping methodology.

6.2   Creating a clear working definition of Innovation
A clear working definition for innovation is necessary as part of a mission statement and to ensure that the organisation sees innovation as a common goal. A definition was attempted in section 2.2.2 and this is repeated here.

> The creation of productive, courageously backed, creative ideas by intelligent, knowledgeable, highly motivated people working in a supportive environment.

At the time it was stated that it maybe possible to improve the definition whilst ensuring that it remains brief. However, it was also stated that it is probably better for individual organisation to consider their own definition. This is true even if, after due consideration, the one above is used. The process of considering the meaning of innovation for 'this' organisation is a worthwhile endeavour.

This definition includes the main points about innovation captured by the statements at the beginning of section. 2.2. Although it does not use the word 'new' within the context of ideas, instead it uses the word 'creative'. It may be that 'new' is more correct but 'creative' seems to provide more encouragement to those involved with the scheme than 'new'. Of course, 'new creative' or 'creative new', could be used instead but I am happy with creative because, whilst it is not intended to exclude ideas that may not be creative, it does imply people that submit ideas are creative.

The word 'productive' is intended to imply that the ideas are successful in that they deliver benefit for the organisation. Words like 'improvement', 'introduction' and even 'exploitation' have been used in the earlier statements where I have used 'productive'. Including 'productive' is intended to show that the ideas are meant for a purpose, they are intended to deliver a goal and the goal is related to success. Whether 'productive' captures all this is debatable, but it is brief.

The phrase 'courageously backed' is intended to show that the organisation must support ideas if they are to be successful. Using the word 'courageously' is intended to show all staff that there are risks involved in backing ideas and the company will do its best to have good ideas adopted although it probably cannot adopt them all.

Using the words 'intelligent' and 'knowledgeable' is recognition of the qualities of the staff within the definition, just as 'courageously backed' includes the role of the organisation. This is intended to give staff a goal to work towards and also intended to congratulate those submitting ideas for their intelligence and knowledge.

Using the word 'motivated' and the phrase 'supportive environment' are both indicators of the working environment and are intended to provide goals for all staff including the managers responsible for the environment. Referring back to section 2.5.3 where comment from various people concerning motivation brought to light the statement "Attitudes are contagious, is yours worth catching?". This statement and others like it reinforce the idea that environment and motivation is not just something that the organisation does, it is up to all staff to contribute.

The definition provided above will then make a reasonable working definition. However, organisations should not be put off either improving it or writing a completely new one, or even using a different one found elsewhere. Whichever definition is used, just make sure that it satisfies a need and understand what need it is intended to satisfy.

6.3 Understanding the goals

The idea of using goals within the innovation process was discussed in section 2.3. The general theme of the discussion considered whether goals would target innovation too closely, leaving the area outside the goals unexplored as far as ideas are concerned. Alternatively, not having goals may mean that the ideas, if there are any generated, may have little to do with business success and may be irrelevant to the business.

Not so long ago there was a series of television advertisements in the UK about a bank that was being portrayed as innovative. The advertisement series showed one very bright employee who produced a range of very innovative and potentially life changing inventions. In each advert, the ideas of that person were ignored until he came up with something that would make the bank more successful, which he did of course, in each advert. This consigned the other inventions, such as, I think I remember this correctly, an anti gravity orb, to the scrap heap.

The point of the advert was fairly clear because the ideas about banking services that the employee came up with were portrayed as new, innovative and excellent services. However, I am not so sure whether the set of adverts actually portrayed the bank as innovative, or quite the opposite. Maybe the fact that I still remember it means that at least the advert was successful but maybe I should be able to remember which bank it was, but I can't.

The point to be made here is that if an organisation has goals for innovation, how tightly controlled should they be and will they exclude ideas that lie outside of these goals. One large manufacturing company in the UK, and probably many others, has a department that deals in intellectual property. The company is keen to use patents to protect innovative new ideas whether they are about its product range or not. This company sees the ideas as having the potential to make profit for the company even if it does not exploit the ideas itself. It is interested in seeing the ideas exploited and earning profit from that exploitation but maybe by contracting the idea to a third party or even selling it on all together. The company may be prepared to provide 'courageous backing' for the idea and yet allow others to exploit it in the practical sense.

In a case like this, staff with good ideas that may lie in completely novel areas, may be encouraged to use the company they work for to develop the idea because the process of patent search etc can be expensive. The company will take the risks associated with this investment and in return will share in the profits from the new idea.

The main part of the discussion concerning goals has been to establish that it is the business goals that are important. However, there has also been considerable discussion that shows that allowing greater freedom of expression within the generation of ideas may be profitable for the organisation. Taking these factors into account, a set of goals for innovation could be considered.

a) To generate ideas that are intended to move the organisation towards its business goals

b) To utilise spare capacity and capitalise on existing resources to create new profitable ventures for the organisation

c) To allow ideas to express their value in intellectual property for the benefit of the organisation and the individual

Goal a, is intended to be the main 'local' goal for the organisation; the organisational driver that leads to improvement and growth. Goal b is intended to ensure the organisation remains open to alternative revenue streams that it may already have the capacity and capability to implement. Goal c is to encourage the organisation to be seen as a mutually profitable way for individuals or teams to express their innovative ideas that may be entirely foreign to the way the organisation normally works; a partnership in innovation between the organisation and its staff.

6.4 Creating a Policy for Innovation
Using the word 'policy' here rather than 'procedure' is intended to imply that innovation is to become an integral part of the organisation, a statement of policy. As part of this, innovation will be a managed policy (section 6.1), it will be properly defined, reflecting the needs and aspirations of the organisation (section 6.2), it will have clear goals (section 6.3) and it will have policy and procedure to provide clear and thorough guidance for all those involved with it.

The process developed in section 3.6.1 seemed to incorporate everything that was needed for innovation, or at least all of the components that have been described. When it is examined again however, the diagram seems to imply that there is no need to generate ideas when measurement is being used. Ideas are only needed when there is no measurement. This is of course, not the case and the diagram needs to be modified to reflect this.

The diagram should show that ideas remain the source for innovation but ideas may come from thought about a process or an activity or they may come when measurements are performed or when the analysis of measurements is made available. It is easy to imagine that a person looking at say production figures for a work cell may see a fall in one particular week that has been duplicated on several occasions in the past. This person may combine what has become known about the production rate with what he or she already knows about something else that happened every time those production rates fell. This combined information plus some creative thinking may lead to a useful idea that could prevent the production rates from periodically falling.

The innovation process diagram should reflect this change.

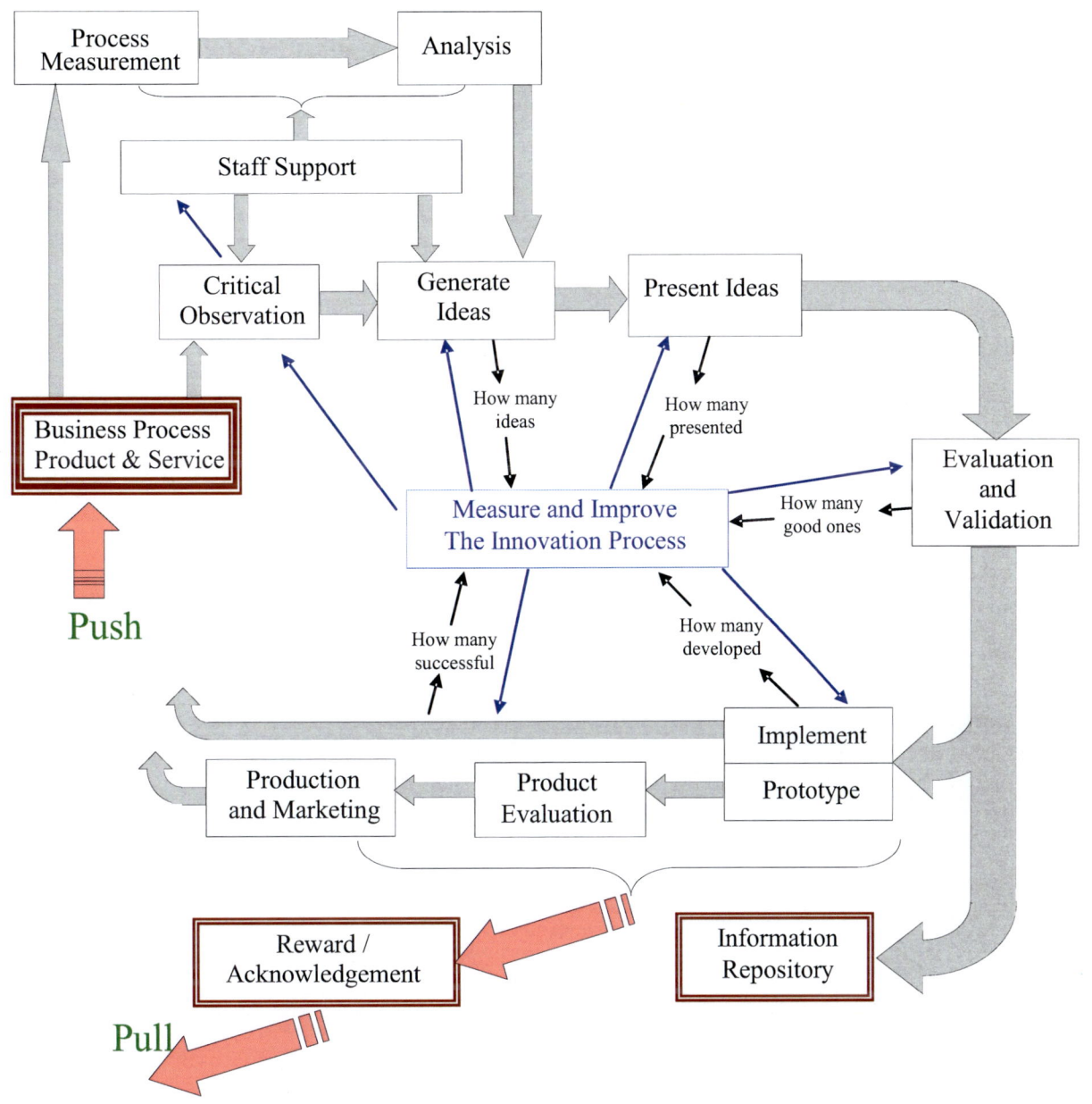

This diagram provides a more realistic beginning for the innovation process showing that ideas can come simply from observation and thought or they could come from any combination of thought and access to process data. The diagram has also been slightly modified to show that the results of the innovation process are intended to be fed back to improve the process.

Even now, this modified diagram only addresses objective a) from section 6.3. The innovation process diagram is shown as gaining its inspiration from the business process (in its general sense) and also supplying improvement to the business process. Objectives or goals b) and c) open the innovation process up so that it can extend beyond the confines of the business process. Whilst it has been argued that this is possibly a desirable state, it is likely the organisation would prefer that most of the effort is devoted to improving the profitability of the core activities of the organisation. For this reason, whilst it may be a good idea to include goals b) and c) and provide the infrastructure that supports them, it may be preferable to leave the diagram shown above as it is, focussing attention on the business process. The innovation manager can then find other ways to make sure all staff know about the wider opportunities within innovation whilst keeping most of the focus on the business process.

In this way, the innovation policy extends beyond that shown in the innovation process diagram. This is a desirable position because it means it is more likely that the innovation process diagram will at some stage be developed and improved to reflect the growing and developing policy and the changing needs of the organisation. The goals set in section 6.3 already allow for considerable growth and change within the organisation as well as for the improvement of core business. The diagram above however, more specifically reflects the needs of the core business.

As with many other business components, the difference between policy and process in this case creates a need for a written policy which covers management, definition, goals and process and is altogether more flexible than the day to day workings of a department needs to be. The innovation department may indeed settle into a stable state that continually develops the business process and this is a desirable situation. However, the responsiveness to the needs for change or attitude to new opportunity is embodied within the innovation policy itself and the responsibility for delivering the policy belongs to the innovation manager.

Clearly the wording of the innovation policy is something that will be a central part of the work of senior organisational managers and directors and of course, the innovation manager. This section has however, discussed at least one way an innovation policy could be formed.

6.4.1 A Written Innovation Policy

The written policy should cover all of the elements of innovation outlined in this book although it can leave out the discussion and justifications which support the decisions made here. It should start with a clear definition for innovation in this particular organisation. The next most important thing to include at the start of the policy document are the objectives of innovation within the context of a particular organisation. Once a definition and objectives are made clear, perhaps with justifications for them included in brief, then the document should make it clear how the innovation policy or scheme is to be implemented and sustained. Implementation will include methods and infrastructure. The process diagram represents one of the methods and the innovation staffing structure, including the head of innovation, represents one part of the infrastructure. Just to make the point perfectly clear, I will include the definition and objectives used in this work below but will not repeat the justifications for their format.

Definition:
The creation of productive, courageously backed, creative ideas by intelligent, knowledgeable, highly motivated people working in a supportive environment.

NOTE: this definition refers primarily to objective a) below. The reader may wish to extend this to cover more aspects of an organisational innovation policy. However, it should be remembered, this definition is simply attempting to define innovation and not the functions of an innovation policy. This constitutes additional information that the written document should address.

Objectives:
  a) To generate ideas which are intended to move the organisation towards its business goals

  b) To utilise spare capacity and capitalise on existing resources to create new profitable ventures for the organisation

  c) To allow ideas to express their value in intellectual property for the benefit of the organisation and the individual

Before moving on with policy document contents, it has already been noted that the process diagram refers mainly to objective a) and the policy should refer to all three objectives. Similarly, the process omits, or at least has no clear statement about, motivation, attitude, culture etc. This simply emphasises the observation that an organisational innovation policy is more than a process even though it may be felt that an efficient, well tuned, innovation process is the chief contributory factor in making an innovative organisation. Without objectives b) and c) there will be holes in the policy and without attending to the human drivers of innovation such as motivation, the process may grind to a halt quite soon after its birth.

Having decided the policy document must address more than the innovation process, the document structure can be considered in more detail. Please remember that this book intends to provide ideas and suggestions without being authoritative. This is a difficult balance to achieve when the desire is also to create something concrete for others to examine and use as they wish. The suggestions made here follow from the justifications provided early on in the book but the conclusions drawn and the structure proposed are intended to make things clear and not intended to represent a correct way of doing things. Please consider the report structure, along with the rest of the book, using a critical eye. That does not mean you should look for places where it is WRONG and places where it may be RIGHT, these concepts are simply not relevant here. The work is trying to help the reader to develop an innovation policy. It is not presenting a policy that is somehow THE RIGHT ONE, and should really be used by everyone.

6.4.2 Policy Document Structure
This section will contain suggestions about how an innovation policy document could be laid out and it will also consider the content of the document in outline.

1) The title of the document, date of creation and list of authors and affiliation
2) A statement explaining the purpose and context of the document and identifying what a potential reader should gain from it
3) A statement about innovation that includes a clear definition of innovation
4) A statement concerning the objectives of innovation that clearly lists a set of objectives
   a. To include a clear justification of, and implementation guide for each objective
5) The Infrastructure for Innovation
   a. The head of innovation
   b. The governing body for innovation (who the head reports to)
   c. The staff, titles and roles
   d. Physical resources including accommodation etc
6) A general statement concerning implementation of the whole policy
7) The innovation process, diagram and implementation description
   a. To include how the process will be implemented, monitored and developed
   b. To include responsibilities of innovation team staff
   c. To include responsibilities for all staff
8) Cultural issues including motivation etc
9) Other process requirements such as support for objectives b) and c)
   a. These objectives are likely to spin off from initial ideas such as an idea to create a new product or an idea that has merit from an intellectual property perspective but that cannot be developed in house. A policy to deal with such issues should be made clear in this section of the document.
10) How the Innovation Policy is intended to affect the business or organisation
   a. For instance, is the organisation expected to become more efficient, to grow, to increase market share, to branch out into new ventures etc, what does success mean for the innovation policy?

A particular organisation or business is likely to have an overall business document format that this structure will need to fit into. The purpose of including the structure is to encourage the reader to think carefully about the content of the innovation policy document. The document itself should be fit for purpose. This means that somebody consulting the document should be able to get guidance concerning the innovation policy and its implementation and sustainability, from the document. The document should be able to function as a guide to the innovation department as well as a more general guide to the whole organisation. It should also contain specific responsibilities so that any employee can consult the innovation policy document to find out what is expected of him or her as far as innovation is concerned.

6.5 Implementing the Policy and Sustaining Innovation

The point made right at the beginning of this chapter was that someone needs to take ownership of and take on responsibility for the innovation scheme or policy. It has been suggested this person will be the innovation manager but this simply shows where the focus of responsibility lies. Innovation is the responsibility of the whole organisation. It requires involvement at the very top of the organisation and also involvement at all staff levels. If the board of directors intend to oversee an innovative organisation then they must discuss innovation, the innovation policy and how well the scheme is performing. The person who supplies data for the board will be the innovation manager.

It was pointed out in section 6.1, staff cannot be forced to innovate but they can be encouraged to do so. They can also be encouraged to see innovation as at least partly their responsibility. The implementation of a policy for innovation requires an effort which is organisation wide. One of the main elements of this organisation wide initiative will be in the creation and maintenance of a business culture, or the term environment for innovation may be preferred. The idea of a business culture and some of the details concerning how it may be implemented and sustained were discussed in chapter 4.

The creation of the right business culture is probably a necessary prerequisite for an innovative organisation operating and sustaining a working policy for innovation. The culture cannot be implemented without support at the very top of the organisation. However, business culture is a long term commitment and an organisation should not wait until it has the right culture before attempting to promote innovation. Rather, the two should be seen as complementary and parallel activities.

The problem with processes that are intended to support managed activities is that they can be the cause of neglect of other areas. In this case, the business culture could be the thing which is neglected. Practical steps to promote a positive business culture or rather environment for innovation were discussed throughout chapter 4.

6.5.1 Implementing the Policy

Clearly, from the discussion, the ideal way to implement a policy for innovation would be to:

1) Appoint an Innovation Manager
2) Create a clear working Definition for Innovation
3) Document the initial Goals of Innovation and Create a Mission Statement or simple long term objective
4) Decide on the initial resource needs of innovation and what the organisation can reasonably afford to invest and create the initial innovation resource
5) Design a Policy for Innovation and create the policy document
6) Take baseline measurements of performance
7) Allow a reasonable lead in time for the scheme
8) Implement the Innovation Monitoring and Improvement element of the process
9) Build Innovation review points into senior management meetings at appropriate times

The innovation manager, whether full or part time, should be involved in the development and implementation of the policy and so should be appointed at an early stage. It may be necessary to obtain some external input at the initial stages to advise the innovation manager if he or she is new to the idea. The innovation manager can later decide whether external support is needed later in the process or if it can now be implemented by internal actions only. One of the most obvious areas which may require external help is in evaluating the initial business culture and considering if and how it should be changed to make it more appropriate to an environment for innovation. An internal manager may not be able to objectively analyse the existing business culture very easily.

The working definition, the goals and mission statement have been dealt with earlier in this chapter. They are repeated in these steps because it is a good idea for the innovation manager to be involved in definitions and goals even if these are set in advance. At least the innovation manager should be given the opportunity to review them and comment on or even modify them.

Deciding on the initial resources to allocate to an innovation policy may be one of the most difficult steps. There may be a tendency to try to make the policy work without any additional resources. This usually involves attempting to utilise existing staff and management time more efficiently. Whilst this may be possible for a small scale scheme, it would be difficult to sustain the policy beyond its initial set up and the policy would be subject to degradation when the other duties of the part time staff become more demanding. The ideal situation would be to create a full time management post along with enough staff posts to operate the scheme. For an innovation scheme to work across a large organisation, this is likely to be an essential resource requirement. Additional physical resources will be needed to service the various elements of the scheme. For instance, computing hardware and software are likely to be needed. If there is to be a suggestion box scheme for instance, then resources will be required for this etc. In other words, the innovation department or group will need a budget.

The policy for innovation should always be reviewed by the innovation manager and if necessary altered. The policy or process discussed in section 6.4 may be too complex, too simplified or simply inappropriate for any specific organisational needs. Considering the policy shown and the reasons that it has been developed in this way should at least cause the innovation manager and others involved to feel it necessary to justify their own approaches to innovation and the decisions that they make about an innovation policy.

Baseline measurements of the business process will be required in order to evaluate the effectiveness of the innovation scheme. This implies that a set of measuring points will need to be finalised early on, even though these may be modified later. Measuring the business process and the innovation process were discussed in section 5.3. For a new innovation scheme, measurements of the initial innovation process are all likely to be zero. However, in some cases, isolated elements of a scheme may have been in place, such as a suggestion box and the outcome of suggestions. If so, these can form the baseline measurements of the innovation process itself.

The lead in time for the innovation policy will be required to allow staff to set up the necessary systems, to promote and explain the scheme to the workforce and to ramp up operations. Even for a large scheme this is not likely to be more than six months but a much shorter time is likely, particularly where the workforce is readily accessible. The lead in time can also be the time during which initial measurements are taken since no actual operations will be in progress. The lead in time should be as short as possible; otherwise any staff involved may become de-motivated by the lack of activity and therefore the lack of progress.

The innovation monitoring process should come on stream as soon as the innovation process itself starts. Also, dates for review by senior managers should be set at the beginning and decisions made as to how frequently review is to be carried out by senior managers. The innovation process itself will be reviewed by the innovation manager and the innovation team but general results from this process will be available for inspection by senior managers and possibly many of them by all staff.

It should be remembered, the innovation process, that will probably form the main area of activity, is not the whole innovation policy. The issues of culture, including attitudes and values, the issues of staff motivation and the issue of environment are all part of the innovation policy and therefore are all elements that an organisation should wish to improve. This means that periodic measurement of culture, motivation and environment should at least be attempted so that progress can be monitored. This issue was discussed in section 4.4 and it was recognised there that this is a difficult thing to achieve. Measurements around the innovation and business processes will be much easier and the data they deliver will be much easier to interpret. However, this should not be allowed to cause the innovation team to neglect culture, motivation and environment. It can be acknowledged however, that the success of the innovation process by delivering significant business benefit can be considered as a strong indicator that culture, motivation and environment are improving; but this should not be taken for granted.

Clearly the innovation policy document will not only consider the measurement of culture, motivation and environment but will explain policy that is to have a positive influence on each. The elements of such a policy have been discussed in section 4 but they should be spelled out clearly in the policy document. Failure to do this will mean that culture, motivation and environment will become a neglected part of the innovation policy and this may have a serious effect on the whole scheme.

6.5.1.1   Individual Innovation Initiatives

In some larger organisations, certain managers may have considerable local authority over one section of the organisation. This manager may see the benefits of innovation for his or her particular working area, before the rest of the organisation does. It is reasonable to conclude that such a manager could carry out the whole process identified in 6.5.1 within his or her local working area.

Clearly the area manager would need to consider how the rest of the organisation may affect the local efforts, but it is likely that in many cases the manager will be able to allow the local innovation policy to work locally, without interference from the global company structure.

This general idea may be considered by large organisations as a way of piloting an innovation scheme rather than attempting an organisation wide policy from the start. Using a local, reasonably isolated pilot could reduce the risks involved in developing a much larger scheme. In addition, any initial problems could be resolved within the pilot before the scheme is allowed to grow into the rest of the organisation.

6.5.2 An Innovation Policy brings Change

Change Management is a separate topic and it is inappropriate to deal with it at length here. However, it should be recognised that the introduction of a policy for innovation will bring changes to the organisation and to the way that staff will work. More than this, it will be desirable to raise the profile of an innovation policy at the right time, as the policy is being prepared. There are some very basic components of change management which are likely to prove very useful when bringing the innovation policy into being. For each of the components identified here, the intention is that all staff should be informed about them. This information dissemination could take the form of a news letter, an intranet page and change email etc.

1) **Clearly State what is being Proposed**
    Explain the introduction of the innovation scheme in the clearest terms. Simply tell staff, the organisation intends to develop an active and successful innovation policy that is to involve all staff. Further explain that staff are the most important part of this policy but the organisation intends to fully support the policy with other resources.

2) **Demonstrate the Need for Change**
    Show why the innovation policy is needed and try to give some examples such as maintaining a competitive advantage or ensuring the longer term success of the company etc. It may, in some cases, be useful to show that without the new policy, the company will operate at a disadvantage in the future. Try to elicit the buy in of all staff.

3) **Explain the Goal**
    Clearly state what the fully working innovation policy will be like and show what it is intended to deliver.

4) **Outline the Plan**
    Outline the plan for the policy in simple and clear terms. This would probably not include details from the policy document but would identify the main elements of the scheme and projected mileposts for their implementation. It may nevertheless be useful for all staff to know there is a policy document and that they can read it if they choose to do so.

5) **Identify the Leaders**

Identify the leaders of the policy and those who will work directly for it. Try to provide contact points so that staff can feel they have immediate access to the scheme even before it is fully operational.

6) **Provide a Communication Platform**

Create a mechanism for periodic updates concerning progress in implementing the innovation policy. This may take the form of a news letter, a series of workshops etc. An organisation may even wish to launch the scheme with some high profile event. Allow any good ideas from staff to influence the policy.

7) **Keep People informed about Progress**

Make sure staff are kept up to date. This means making sure that news does not dry up and that progress is not seen to decline.

There are two main reasons these things are important. The first is, the innovation scheme is to involve all staff and therefore they need to know about it and be fully informed and ready for it when it is introduced. The second reason is to help the scheme leaders and organisers to clarify their plans simply and clearly so that they can be explained. This process will help ensure the policy is a workable policy that can be easily followed. If the policy is too complicated to be explained simply, then it seems unlikely it will work properly.

6.5.3 A Sustainable Policy

Sustaining the innovation policy will be as difficult as sustaining any policy which is not directly involved with production or service delivery. In such cases, there will always be a tendency to slacken off or loosen control. The key to sustaining the policy should be built into the very structure of the policy in the first place. The setting up of goals, or measuring points or review and monitoring points, will all create the feel of an on going rather than a fleeting policy.

It may be difficult to aim for simply sustaining a policy like innovation. The policy of innovation will have been designed to improve things. It is therefore reasonable that sustaining the policy is not the real goal; the real goal will be the constant improvement of it. Occasionally, things will take a knock, maybe as a result of pressures or events from outside the organisation. However, the scheme should be able to recover from such events, take stock of where they have left it and continue to improve, or begin to improve again, from that point.

At the bottom line, the innovation policy should be able to show gradual and sustained improvement in the business. The measurement processes set up at the beginning of the scheme should be able to show the correlation between activity within the innovation scheme and improvement of the business process. Clearly, periodic monitoring and control of this is absolutely essential in sustaining the policy. The idea that occasionally, the innovation scheme should generate a massive innovation that may have large scale business implications should not be ruled out. It will be important, through the maintenance of proper records, that such innovation can at least in part, be attributed to the activities of the innovation scheme.

Sustainability is also likely to be influenced by the factors which were discussed in section 4.9. Making the innovation scheme happen and then continuing to make it happen will be issues that will be promoted by a good business culture, a well designed scheme, adequate resources, well targeted measurement and well informed, highly motivated leaders.

One of the key elements in sustaining the innovation scheme will be success.

6.6 Should Managers Innovate?

The main theme of the discussions developed here has been innovation but primarily the management of innovation. It would be easy to understand from this that managers should manage the environment and the process of innovation and it is really up to others to actually have innovative ideas. However, managers often have a more global view of a situation and this can put them in a better position to have innovative ideas about the business process or about innovation itself.

The question asked here, "Should managers innovate?", can most certainly be answered in the affirmative. A manager should not be excluded from the innovation process, but should interact with it as any other member of staff is expected to do. The point made above is that it may be reasonable to expect a relatively greater number of ideas to come from managers than from other operational staff. This seems to be a perfectly reasonable expectation, managers are often more experienced, more confident in making suggestions and as already stated, have an overview of a process which can allow them to see potential problems that others cannot see.

There is no general reason why managers should use a separate mechanism to submit ideas. However, if the expectation that managers should have more ideas than operational staff is to be tested, then the records of idea submission etc should show whether the person submitting the idea is a manager. The detail with which this is done may in turn allow the innovation assessment process to see what sorts of people are submitting the most ideas as well as which individuals. Are all of the ideas coming from the managers, operational staff, administrators, technicians etc? This may be useful information and could lead to improvements in the process in general.

Summary

An organisation looking for support with the design and implementation of an innovation policy that has every chance of being highly successful may wish to start by looking for someone else who has done it before and then copying what they did. This approach may be seen as one which reduces the risks of making resources available for a project and increasing the likelihood of success and therefore payback and profit. There are a number of problems with this approach, the first one being whether the claims made for the highly successful example can be completely believed. When people report on an event, a project or other activity, they tend to do so with some goal in mind and it is often very difficult to be completely objective. For instance, when reporting on a funded project, a project funded by say a government body, everyone concerned is looking for success. Failure means that the funding agency may have spent public money unwisely and therefore may be criticised, failure means that the lead organisation may have been less than fully competent and therefore may not get more funding in future, failure means that the project leader did not do a good job and his or her reputation may suffer, failure means that the project team were not up to the task and this may affect promotion prospects etc. Failure means negative things for everyone involved, particularly those writing the report.

The point being made here is not that all reports are a fabrication, simply that they should be read to extract information from but not believed verbatim. Within the context of innovation, the argument made here is that the organisation which desires a successful innovation programme should put effort into its design and implementation and be prepared to review and improve it over time. Looking for a quick fix may lead to the selection of the wrong thing or at least something which won't work in every particular case. Even growing an innovation programme from smaller scale initiatives may work in certain cases. However, in such cases, there may be barriers present that could prevent smaller scale initiatives from ever growing into successful schemes.

The first chapter of this book considered interviews, discussion, meetings, workshops etc held with people that all had a strong interest in innovation from an organisational perspective. The information was presented as discussion rather than evidence, to be agreed with or challenged by the reader. However, within the discussion, there were elements of common agreement that present opinions which seem to be more generally held. Discussion is a useful place to begin a programme of innovation development. There may be many people within an organisation with experience and valid opinion concerning innovation who may help in the design of a programme that could be extremely well suited to a particular organisation. The discussion provided in chapter 1 will make an interesting reference point with which new opinion and experience may be compared. At least the opinion can be considered as it stands and discussed to establish if it will work 'here'.

The focus of the discussion on innovation was the benefit to the company or organisation. It was not an academically led discussion about theory but a workplace biased discussion about practice. Several of the elements of innovation that became central in later chapters were raised in the early discussion. Certainly the most pronounced element was that of motivation which is itself linked very strongly to environment and culture. For me, the most memorable part of the discussion, certainly the most memorable part of interviews and meetings, were the items which were discussed under the heading of memorable comment. Most if not all of these were simply comments made by or positions taken by individuals within the context of a discussion about innovation. They are memorable because they appear to me at least, to be highly relevant to the practical task of promoting innovation within an organisation. They are also things which can be used to test other views against practicality.

The second and rightly, the largest chapter was chapter 2 with its direct focus on innovation. It may seem odd to have a book about innovation with one chapter out of six, being about innovation. Perhaps the converse is more interesting, that five of the six chapters were focused on something other than innovation. The early part of chapter 2 considered some of the more distant parts of innovation such as memory and attention. In earlier work, these more remote parts were given much more space than they are here because they are so important if people are to really begin to understand innovation. Everyone in organisations seems to want the most efficient delivery of anything that they undertake. So for an innovation policy, maybe a one day training course would be considered useful. I hope after reading this book that you don't still think this way. But whatever people think, there are still real pressures to get things done efficiently. As discussed earlier, the problem with this is often in the way efficiency is measured, not that looking for efficiency is in itself incorrect. If understanding that human memory may be less than perfect and understanding a little more about what it is good at and what it is not so good at, can help to sustain innovation, then it may be worthwhile in the longer term. The more distant parts of innovation may not need to be addressed up front but may be better addressed as an on going part of the promotion and maintenance of the scheme.

Innovation is another of those concepts used within business that is very widely used but very poorly understood, at least from a definition perspective. When people can't agree on definitions, the argument that it does not really matter what it means as long as we all do it, seems to surface. This argument is often used with Knowledge Management when people can't really agree what knowledge is. But within an organisation at least, it does matter that everyone has a common understanding of what innovation is and what its goals are etc. To suggest otherwise is surely sowing the seeds of confusion. Even if it is difficult to form a common understanding of the concept, this does not mean that it should be avoided.

Chapter two also discussed the potential innovators and how they are to be developed. This is where motivation featured as a core theme within innovation and of the environment for innovation and the culture of the organisation. There is a considerable body of research concerning various aspects of motivation. However, most of the practical discussion focused on practical things which can be done to help to encourage motivation. After all, whatever is known about the theories, it is the practical and successful ideas which will make a difference to the policy. Like a knowledge of memory and attention however, at least a general understanding of the theories of motivation will probably be of value. Again, just as for the other more distant elements of innovation, this understanding of motivation is something that can be developed during the programme of innovation as part of the effort to improve it. An important section of chapter 2 concerned the most directly relevant part of the discussion, that of having ideas. To show that having ideas is possibly the core theme of innovation and then to neglect to do anything at all about helping people to have ideas, is almost certainly to overlook a significant opportunity.

The process for innovation addressed in chapter 3 may form the heart of an organisational innovation policy. This is because it provides things to actually do each day, things to measure and test and a general direction. The process considered along with goals and mission statements can clarify the activities which will be carried out in an innovation scheme. Of the two earlier examples of a policy shown, both had merits but could probably be improved. The new policy, offered as an improvement was an attempt to embody the activities of an innovation programme whilst retaining the brevity needed from a set of guidelines.

Chapter 4 showed that the process could not really be considered effectively without considering the environment for innovation. Rather than environment however, this chapter spent most of its time discussing organisational culture. The justification for this is that the environment relates very closely to the way people behave within it. If people are happy and positive, friendly and constructive, then the environment is likely to look much better than if everyone is miserable, negative, hostile, and destructive. However, chapter 4 did spend some of its time discussing other ways, other than culture, that the environment itself could be made more conducive to innovation. One of the key observations about organisational culture is that changing it is not, definitely not, a short term project. An innovation scheme should not wait for the organisation to first establish the most favourable culture and environment that it possibly can. The innovation project must get under way and the business culture and environment for innovation must be developed in parallel with the innovation scheme.

It was claimed, at least indirectly, the key to sustaining the innovation policy was probably assessing and evaluating it. Chapter 5 considered the assessment of innovation and discussed two innovation analysers which were developed to assist organisations that were looking to cultivate an innovation policy. The value of assessment and evaluation is that it inevitably leads to the desire for constant improvement; at least it does with the right attitudes or culture in place. The idea of considering innovation as Continuous Improvement, as introduced in the knowledge study project discussed in section 3.1.2, demands that things are measured. If they are not measured, then how is anyone to know when things are improving?

Although the analysers discussed in chapter 4 were actually considered to be very useful, the sort of measurement needed to sustain an innovation process is more focused and based on justifiable data rather than opinion. Opinion is of course valuable but there needs to be data in this case to drive the innovation process forward. Inevitably, measurements can indicate a focus of activity where it is not really desired. This can be a problem with some objective measuring schemes and therefore needs to be allowed for during the design of the scheme.

The final chapter, chapter 6, took the information from previous chapters and focused this towards the goal of creating, managing and sustaining the innovation policy in an organisation. It was not really the intention in chapter 6 to provide a blueprint which organisations could or should use to implement their own innovation policy but it was the intention to provide more concrete ideas to help organisations to design the best policy that they can. In addition, the intention was to show that once an organisation has designed and implemented a policy, it should then seek to improve it and move it closer to the needs of the organisation. The point that innovation is about change was not lost and means that an innovation policy must be able to adapt to changes and even recover from disaster. Wherever the policy finds itself at any particular point, the desire should always be to make it better, more useful to the organisation. Making innovation work means that innovation is making the organisation work.

Sources and Influences

This book was written between December 2006 and August 2008 as part of the development of an Innovation program for AKRI Limited. The experiences gained by the author that enabled this work to be constructed have been derived from a number of projects and have been informed by a number of individuals and companies. Since the information contained in this book has been created from work with so many people and organisations, it is regrettably possible that I will omit the indirect contributions made by some. However, I will attempt to acknowledge the sources which have influenced this work. Unfortunately, I cannot include the names of most of the individuals here because of the difficulty of contacting many of them so long after their contribution was made.

Some of these influences date back to the early 1990s and those individuals who made them may not be located in the same organisations and some organisation names may have changed.

Blackburn College Senior Management Team between 1990 and 2004
Blackburn Borough Council
European ADAPT Project + European Partners
European ESF Funding
European ERDF Funding
UK DTI Support and Funding
BAE Systems Samlesbury and Warton
Rolls-Royce plc
Akzo Nobel Decorative Coatings
Coop-Bank
TDS CAD Graphics
Worswick Engineering
NORWEB
Scapa Scandia Ltd
Lancashire Constabulary
St.Helens RLFC
Wigan RLFC
Blackburn Health Service
Enterprise pc
University of Central Lancashire
Precision Polymer Engineering
Warwick & Bailey Ltd
Imperial Home Décor Group (UK) Ltd

Also thanks to:
Lee Jorgensen MD Funzig Web Design
Martin Holden

With special thanks to departed friends:
Robert Muller
Rob Milne MD Intelligent Applications

Reading List:
Your Memory A User's Guide – Alan Baddeley – 1993
Thinking and Reasoning – Alan Garnham & Jane Oakhill – 1996
Motivation and Personality – Abraham H. Maslow - 1970
Journey to the Centers of the Mind – Susan A. Greenfield – 1995
These books are mentioned explicitly in the text. Many other books have influenced this work indirectly. Topics including Artificial Intelligence, The Human Mind, Philosophy, particularly Epistemology, Truth and Reasoning, have had a strong influence. Business influence has come directly from company involvement.